100
THINGS
THEY DON'T
WANT YOU
TO
KNOW

For Rosie and Lottie

100 THINGS THEY DON'T WANT YOU TO KNOW

The World's Greatest Conspiracies and Unsolved Crimes

Daniel Smith

Quercus

First published in Great Britain in 2015 by Quercus Editions Ltd

This paperback edition published in 2017 by

Quercus Editions Ltd
Carmelite House
50 Victoria Embankment
London EC4Y 0DZ

An Hachette UK company

Editorial by Pikaia Imaging

A CIP catalogue record for this book is available
from the British Library

ISBN 9781786488503

10 9 8 7 6 5 4 3 2 1

Typeset by e-type

Printed and bound in Great Britain by Clays Ltd, St Ives plc

CONTENTS

Introduction   1

CRIMES AND CONSPIRACIES

1   The lost cosmonauts   8
2   The secret mission of Rudolf Hess   10
3   The Zinoviev Letter   13
4   The Baker Street bank job   16
5   The Lynmouth Flood   18
6   Starlite   21
7   The Bilderberg Group   23
8   Stuxnet   26
9   MKUltra   29
10 The Georgia Guidestones   32
11 The Majestic 12   35
12 The Black Sox Scandal   37
13 The Katyn Forest massacre   39
14 The Isabella Stewart Gardner Museum thefts   41
15 Liston vs Ali   43
16 The Irish Crown Jewels   45
17 The Protocols of the Elders of Zion   47

MYSTERY MESSAGES

18 The Voynich Manuscript   52
19 The lost literature of the Maya   55
20 The Kryptos code   57

21	The Shugborough inscription	59
22	Rosslyn Chapel	62
23	The Easter Island glyphs	65
24	The Sego Canyon petroglyphs	67
25	The Third Secret of Fátima	69

DISAPPEARANCES AND VANISHINGS

26	The lost village at Anjikuni Lake	72
27	The disappearance of Judge Crater	74
28	Jimmy Hoffa	77
29	The Valentich incident	80
30	Jean Spangler	82
31	Ambrose Bierce	85
32	Buster Crabb – missing in action	88
33	The Princes in the Tower	91
34	The MV *Joyita*	94
35	The missing Nazi gold	97
36	Glenn Miller	100
37	Louis Le Prince	102
38	Agatha Christie – the lady vanishes	104
39	Jim Thompson	106
40	Arthur Cravan	108

MURDER MOST FOUL AND DEATHS UNACCOUNTABLE

41	The Black Dahlia murder	112
42	The Dyatlov Pass incident	115
43	The severed feet of the northwest seaboard	118
44	The strange death of Edgar Allan Poe	120
45	Michael Faherty – up in flames?	123
46	The 'Boy in the Box'	126
47	Who was Jack the Ripper?	128

48 The death of Lee Harvey Oswald 131

49 Alfred Loewenstein 133

50 The assassination of Olof Palme 135

51 Roberto Calvi – God's banker 138

52 The Borden Murders 141

53 On the Zodiac trail 143

54 The Somerton Man 145

55 The tragedy at Mayerling 147

56 Kaspar Hauser – man of mysteries 149

57 Robert Maxwell – accident at sea? 151

STRANGE ENCOUNTERS

58 The alien autopsy video 154

59 The Marfa lights 156

60 The Comte de Saint Germain 158

61 Spring-Heeled Jack 161

62 *El Chupacabra* 164

63 Who are the Men in Black? 166

64 The mystery of Mercy Brown 169

65 The Mothman 172

66 The *Flying Dutchman* 174

67 The Colares Island UFO wave 176

68 A beast on Bodmin Moor? 178

69 The Minnesota Iceman 180

FORBIDDEN HISTORY

70 Lewis Carroll's lost diaries 184

71 The fate of the *Ourang Medan* 186

72 The naming of America 188

73 Bimini Road 190

74 The Dancing Plague 192

75	The attack on Pearl Harbor	194
76	Elizabethan offspring?	197
77	The crystal skulls	199
78	The Aiud artefact	202
79	The age of the Sphinx	204
80	Shakespeare's true identity	206
81	The Baghdad Battery	209
82	Queen Victoria and John Brown	211
83	Why build Stonehenge?	214
84	Ancient contact with the New World	217
85	The Tarim Mummies	219
86	The Baigong Pipes	222
87	The Man in the Iron Mask	224
88	The bog bodies of Northern Europe	226
89	The Piri Reis map	228
90	The Philadelphia Experiment	230
91	The Turin Shroud	233

FRONTIERS OF SCIENCE

92	The 'Wow!' signal	238
93	Nazi UFOs?	240
94	The Taos Hum	242
95	The disappearing bees	244
96	Thorium fission	246
97	Red Rain	248
98	The Bloop	250
99	The Tunguska Event	252
100	The End of the World	255

Index	258

INTRODUCTION

'Secrecy, being an instrument of conspiracy, ought never to be the system of a regular government.'

Jeremy Bentham

'Truth is what your contemporaries let you get away with.'

Richard Rorty

Everybody loves a mystery – those puzzles that are difficult, and perhaps even impossible, to understand or explain. Consider some of the synonyms that we have for the very word itself: enigma, conundrum, riddle, secret. Each rolls off the tongue and excites the imagination, enticing us with the promise of revelation.

The love of mystery is as strong today as it has ever been. One need only look at the television schedules and bookstores for evidence of our lust for detective fiction, true-life crime and political conspiracy. It is telling, too, that perhaps the greatest mystery-solver of all time, the fictional detective Sherlock Holmes, has enjoyed a remarkable new lease of life since the turn of the century, starring in big budget movies and television series and providing plentiful subject matter for authors, journalists and academics. Our passion for mystery is alive and well.

Yet if truth be told, sometimes it is the quest for resolution that brings more pleasure than uncovering the solution itself.

How often, for instance, does an unidentified, shadowy criminal overlord lose his appalling mystique once he has been unmasked as some grudge-filled social inadequate? Similarly, what great historical teasers have eventually rendered the most disappointing and unsatisfying of explanations? Events and occurrences that once seemed the product of dastardly scheming and devilish intent so often turn out in fact to have been the result of fluke, incompetence or ungoverned malice.

The urge to explore mysteries is a fundamental component of our human nature. In essence, every mystery produces a nick or dint in the veneer of our collective existence and our natural inclination is to hammer them out. The bigger the dint and the longer it's been there, the more fascinating it becomes to us, and the greater the desire to solve it. But we should not always be so hasty – an imperfect veneer is merely evidence of age and experience and is often far more captivating than the one utterly unmarked. All of which is to say, when investigating a mystery, enjoy the journey as it may prove more delightful than the destination.

In some respects, our own time does not seem well suited to birthing truly great mysteries. In a world where 'openness' and 'transparency' are watchwords for the political and commercial elites, there is ostensibly less room for secrecy and mystery. And when governments attempt to shield their actions from public view, there is an army of internet warriors – epitomized by Julian Assange and his WikiLeaks operation – on hand to expose them to the world. Even our celebrity culture has moved away from a focus on mystique towards unbounded revelation. In a world where a celebrity attempts to 'break the internet' by exposing her bottom to anyone who cares to look, one might wonder if mystery has received its death knell!

But let us not be too hasty. For all the talk of openness and connectivity, mystery continues to surround us. Indeed, the more globally interconnected we become, the easier it is to miss some of the links between us. So it is that ideologues plot and perpetrate atrocities undetected, and passenger jets fall from the sky without explanation, and international banks covertly aid their clients to hide their ill-gotten gains. To say nothing of the murder victim who lies dead for weeks before a neighbour notices anything wrong.

So the modern information age does not guarantee unfettered access to the truth after all. We live in an intriguing age in which we receive a constant drip-feed of data in volumes without precedent, but all the while our distrust of what we are told grows. While a world without trust may be a pretty hollow place, it is beholden upon us to vigilantly assess all the information that comes our way. What does it mean? Who's telling us it is so? What axes do they have to grind? These are undoubtedly key questions for the social-networking, rolling-news, Wikipedia generation.

Yet sometimes it is all but impossible to know where truth ends and gives way to inaccuracy – whether offered up in good faith or not. In this grey area, we are left with plenty of delicious doubt and mystery. While it may not always be a comfortable place to reside, it is more often than not hugely interesting.

The 100 cases described in this book are mined from this murky region and comprise a heady cocktail of grand conspiracies, unsolved crimes, unexplained natural phenomena and bewildering historical mysteries. In each instance, two or more theories battle it out to explain what really occurred, yet never can we be definitively sure which is right. It is a task further complicated by the suspicion that many of the arguments are propounded not in the interests of establishing truth, but to deliberately deceive, confuse and obfuscate.

It may be a government wishing to cover its dirty tracks, or a criminal mastermind attempting to evade identification. Equally, there may be a financial incentive to mislead, a wish to save face and calm public fears, or a desire to promote a particular personal agenda. Sometimes, it might merely be that a great practical joke is afoot. The trouble with lies is that they are sometimes just too tempting to spin!

However, we should perhaps be wary of becoming too cynical. It may be that some of the mysteries described herein really do have the simple and innocent explanations that some would have you believe. Indeed, on occasion we perhaps credit our masters with intelligence and acumen they don't deserve, when we accuse them of orchestrating elaborate deceits requiring extensive conspiracies of silence that endure for years, decades or even centuries.

Take, for instance, the notorious conspiracy theory that says Neil Armstrong's Moon landing was faked. While – as we shall see – the Cold War era gave rise to an extraordinary number of sometimes quite preposterous deceptions by the powers-that-be, is it really credible that the US government coordinated such a stunt? Given the number of people that would have been required to execute it and then stay quiet about their activities for years afterwards, this author for one doubts it very much. (It should, however, be noted that Armstrong himself was an advocate for a little speculative mystery in our universe, citing it as one of the forces that drives our species forward. In his words: 'Mystery creates wonder and wonder is the basis of man's desire to understand.')

Even that arch conspiracy theorist, film director Oliver

Stone, has conceded: '. . . not all of life is a result of conspiracy by any means! Accident occurs alongside conspiracy.' It is a notion backed by *Washington Post* columnist Charles Krauthammer, who expressed it thus: 'Whenever you're faced with an explanation of what's going on in Washington, the choice between incompetence and conspiracy, always choose incompetence.' Nonetheless, it is worth being on our guard whenever we are presented with apparently 'conclusive evidence' and 'the true story'. To paraphrase a famous maxim, just because I am paranoid doesn't mean they are telling me the truth . . .

At the very least I hope that the mysteries you are about to dive into will fascinate and entertain. Immerse yourself in them and revel in the thrill that accompanies the pursuit of truth. And rest assured you are in good company – no less an intellectual and philosophical giant than Albert Einstein once acknowledged: 'The most beautiful thing we can experience is the mysterious.'

And if the cases detailed in the pages that follow pique your interest to such an extent that you go on to discover the genuine, irrefutable truth behind them, then so much the better. Let me know if you do. Just don't expect me to believe you . . .

CRIMES AND CONSPIRACIES

1 THE LOST COSMONAUTS

It is easy to forget how fierce competition between the Soviet Union and the United States was at the height of the Cold War. In this clash of ideologies, everything from the Olympics to chess championships became a battleground – and so, of course, did the race to put humans into space. But in their desire to steal a lead, did Moscow cover up the deaths of numerous members of its space programme?

While America claimed the glory of the first manned Moon landing when Neil Armstrong took his 'giant leap for mankind' in 1969, the USSR had previously led the Space Race, launching the first satellite in 1957 and firing Yuri Gagarin into orbit in 1961. But there have long been rumours that at least two earlier attempts at putting a man in orbit ended in tragedy and cover-up.

The earliest claims of unacknowledged fatalities are said to have come from a Czech government official with links to the West. However, reports of earlier manned launches were dismissed by Gagarin himself as rumours resulting from test flights involving dummies and human voice recordings. Another version of events claimed that Vladimir Ilyushin beat Gagarin into space by a few days but then crash-landed in China, where he was held for over a year. Moscow, the theory goes, hushed up events in order to avoid a diplomatic incident.

Some of the most compelling evidence for 'lost cosmonauts' came from Italian brothers and radio hams Achille and Gian Judica-Cordiglia, who tuned in to Soviet space missions in the early 1960s from a base near Turin. Over several years, they claimed, they listened in on many extraordinary episodes, including at least three in which cosmonauts were literally dying somewhere in orbit. While the brothers have their sceptics, their activities certainly brought them to the attention of both Soviet and Italian security services.

It is, of course, quite possible that tales of dead Russians in space were spread by those with anti-Moscow agendas (or even by fantasists craving attention). In the post-Soviet era, no conclusive evidence has emerged despite the opening of state archives. On the other hand, we know that much sensitive material was lost or purposely destroyed during the Communist regime's long collapse. Given the lengths to which both the White House and the Kremlin went to preserve secrecy amidst the paranoia of the Cold War, tales of lost cosmonauts are all too credible, even if unproven.

2 THE SECRET MISSION OF RUDOLF HESS

In 1941, Hitler's deputy in the Nazi hierarchy flew himself on an apparently unsanctioned mission to Scotland in a bid to secure peace with Britain. Subsequently arrested and convicted at the Nuremberg Trials, Rudolf Hess was jailed in Berlin's Spandau Prison until his suicide in 1987. But did Hess really kill himself? And was Spandau's last prisoner even really Hess anyway?

Born in 1894, Rudolf Hess fought in the First World War, and not long after fell under the spell of a little-known, Austrian-born political firebrand called Adolf Hitler. In 1923, the two men stood shoulder to shoulder as the nascent Nazi party attempted a coup in Berlin that became known as the Beer Hall Putsch. Hess received a prison sentence of 18 months and while in jail helped Hitler compose his gospel of hate, *Mein Kampf*.

In 1933, shortly after Hitler had taken power in Germany, Hess was named deputy leader of the Nazis. By the time the Second World War broke out, he was second in line to succeed Hitler as national leader. Having given himself over to the Führer so entirely for most of his adult life, his actions in 1941 are thus all the more surprising.

It has traditionally been thought that Hess was concerned Germany could not win a war on two fronts.

With the invasion of Russia imminent, he decided to take matters into his own hands and try to make peace with Britain. Having received his pilot's licence in the late 1920s, he prepared a Messerschmitt 110 aircraft to fly to Scotland. There he planned to meet the Duke of Hamilton, whom he had been incorrectly led to believe was receptive to a peace plan. Hess was to offer Britain unhindered sovereignty over its extant empire in return for its non-intervention in continental Europe.

He embarked on his escapade on the evening of 10 May 1941, taking off from an airfield in Bavaria. Flying fast and low in a bid to avoid being spotted, he made it to Scotland, but had trouble locating Dungavel House, home of the Duke. A little after 11 o'clock, with his plane dangerously low on fuel, he parachuted to safety and was promptly discovered by a farmer who handed him over to the local Home Guard. From there he was taken into police custody. His true identity having then been established, he spent the rest of the war under guard at various locations around the UK.

After the War, Hess was among the first defendants to appear before the International Military Tribunal at Nuremberg. Found guilty of conspiracy and crimes against peace, he was given a life sentence to be served at Spandau Prison in West Berlin. By the mid-1960s he was the only inmate of a jail that had facility for up to 600 prisoners. On 17 August 1987, the 93-year-old Hess was found dead in a summer house in the prison grounds, having apparently garrotted himself with a lamp cord suspended from a window frame.

This curious demise opened up many questions. His lawyers and members of his family seriously doubted that he had the physical strength to kill himself in the manner described. His 'suicide note', they further argued, was a missive written some two decades earlier when he feared he was about to succumb to failing health. One theory suggested that the Gorbachev-era Soviet Union was about to agree to Hess's release and British security services, fearful of what he would reveal about the conduct of the Westminster government during the War, had him killed before he could speak out.

There were other equally bold claims. A doctor who examined Spandau's last inmate claimed he lacked the tell-tale wounds that Hess was known to have suffered in the First World War. Had the British substituted an innocent third party for Hess decades earlier? If so, why? Was it to cover up the fact that the real Hess had met some unedifying end? Or had he, as some have suggested, been whisked out of the country to safety elsewhere by members of the British establishment sympathetic to his cause? Others have suggested that Hess never came to Britain at all, but that Berlin had sent a decoy for reasons best known to themselves. Had Hitler wanted to sue for peace but come up with an elaborate ruse in the event of the British government rejecting 'Hess's' advances?

Clearly, there were – and perhaps still are – parties with good reason to fear the truth about Hess's mission coming out. Yet they need not worry unduly, since the official files that offer us the best chance of getting to the bottom of events have either been destroyed or are yet to be scheduled for any kind of public release.

3 THE ZINOVIEV LETTER

Such was the fear of Bolshevism in the 1920s that Britain's first Labour government blamed its 1924 electoral defeat on hysteria thrown up by a forged letter. Ostensibly a note from the Communist International to the British Communist Party calling for agitation within the UK, the 'Zinoviev Letter' was printed by two newspapers just days before the UK's leading socialist party suffered a landslide defeat.

The letter, supposedly from Grigory Zinoviev (head of the Executive Committee of the Communist International in Moscow), came to public attention just as the two nations' governments were attempting to finalize a trade agreement. In the UK, Ramsay MacDonald had become Labour's first prime minister a year earlier and the pact he had negotiated was strongly opposed by the opposition Conservative Party. In early October 1924, MacDonald's minority government lost a confidence vote and new elections were scheduled for 29 October.

As a socialist, MacDonald attracted the opprobrium of much of the British establishment and had powerful enemies. The Zinoviev letter was leaked to the press by persons unknown and printed by the *Daily Mail* on 25 October, just four days before the general election. A particularly damning part of the letter referred to 'revolutionizing of the international and British proletariat'. The *Mail*, never one to play down a story, ran with the headline: 'Civil War Plot by Socialists' Masters: Moscow Orders To Our Reds; Great Plot Disclosed'.

Within two days, Zinoviev himself denied any role in the creation of the letter, stating: 'The letter of 15th September, 1924, which has been attributed to me, is from the first to the last word, a forgery.' MacDonald himself smelled a rat too, noting in a speech at the time, '. . . how can I avoid the suspicion – I will not say the conclusion – that the whole thing is a political plot?' Nevertheless, Labour was slaughtered at the polls on 29 October and Stanley Baldwin's Conservatives formed a new government. How much did the letter damage Labour's chances? The party was always going to struggle to win, but the mysterious epistle may well have hammered the final nails into its coffin. Perhaps more damagingly, it led to a period of increased tension between the UK and the USSR just as it had appeared that the two countries might come to an accommodation.

Baldwin established a cabinet committee to look into the affair, which concluded that the letter was genuine after all. There would be no further official investigation for decades. However, in 1967 a group of *Sunday Times* journalists published the results of their research into the episode and declared that the letter was a forgery after all, probably created by a band of pro-monarchist Russians working out of Berlin in a bid to weaken Anglo-Russian relations. They also alleged the participation of Conservative Party and intelligence community figures in the conspiracy.

In 1998, a year after Tony Blair had returned the Labour Party to government following 18 years out of office, Foreign Secretary Robin Cook announced a new investigation based on unprecedented access to official records. Gill Bennett, chief historian of the Foreign and Commonwealth Office, published her findings the following year, having trawled the archives of the Foreign Office, MI5 and MI6, as well as state agencies in Russia.

Although she was unable to say exactly who had produced the letter, Bennett too believed it to have been forged, probably by White Russian émigrés in Berlin or perhaps Riga. Even more damaging, though, were her revelations that senior figures within MI5 and/or MI6 were instrumental in leaking the letter to the Conservatives, despite their knowledge that it was not genuine. Desmond Morton (a senior MI6 figure and confidante of Winston Churchill), and Major Joseph Ball of MI5 (and later, of Conservative Central Office) came under particular scrutiny. Stuart Menzies, who would become head of MI6, was meanwhile implicated in supplying the letter to the *Daily Mail*.

Bennett also found that the security services had deliberately misled the Foreign Office over the provenance of the letter, by wilfully claiming that it had come from reliable sources within Moscow when it knew this was far from the case. For instance, just a week after Baldwin's Foreign Secretary Austen Chamberlain had reported that the specially formed cabinet committee was 'unanimously of opinion that there was no doubt as to the authenticity of the Letter', Morton was writing to MI5 that 'we are firmly convinced this actual thing is a forgery'.

A tale, then, that goes to prove that dirty tricks within the security services is by no means a modern-day phenomenon.

4 THE BAKER STREET BANK JOB

It was an audacious robbery at a central London bank and netted the perpetrators a vast fortune, assisted by a good dose of official bungling. But after an initial media frenzy, there was precious little comment about the crime and word went round that the government wanted the heist hushed up. What was it about the events of that night that was not fit for public consumption?

I n a plot reminiscent of the Sherlock Holmes story, 'The Red-Headed League', a gang of robbers rented a shop a couple of doors down from Lloyds Bank on the junction of Marylebone Road and Baker Street. Over a number of weekends, they dug a tunnel and on 11 September 1971 broke through to the bank's vaults. Extraordinarily, a local radio ham picked up communications between the robbers and informed police – but he was unable to specify the location of the bank. The police thus searched 700 sites in central London, including the one under attack, but failed to notice anything amiss. The robbers were able to make off with some £3 million (close to £30 million in today's prices) in cash and valuables plundered from over 250 security boxes.

As might be expected, the press leapt on such a sensational story but after a few days, coverage went strangely quiet. Many Fleet Street editors subsequently claimed that a D-notice – a government order imposing a media gag – had been put in place. Some believed this was to avoid embarrassing stories of police incompetence, but others suspected there was more to it than that. D-notices were usually reserved for coverage of events that threatened national security, not to save the blushes of local bobbies.

In the years since, there has been much speculation about what might have been contained within those vaults that sent MI5 and senior government officials into a spin. Four men were subsequently convicted for the theft and one of them suggested the robbers were shocked to find significant amounts of weaponry and pornography among their haul. Others, though, believe the real cause for concern was a set of indiscreet photos of a leading public figure, which may have subsequently fallen into the possession of a leading agitator in the Black Power movement. It is nonetheless a theory that remains unproven. During the robbery, the thieves sprayed the bank's vault with the cheeky slogan, 'Let Sherlock Holmes try to solve this'. It is a sentiment that remains pertinent to this day.

5 THE LYNMOUTH FLOOD

Lynmouth, on the outskirts of Exmoor in the English county of Devon, was described by artist Thomas Gainsborough as 'the most delightful place for a landscape painter this country can boast'. But in 1952 the village was the epicentre of floods that killed 34 people. It later emerged that government scientists had been carrying out experiments nearby to spur rainfall – was their tampering with nature responsible?

Exmoor, a vast expanse of moorland, was already water-logged when, on 15 December 1952, torrential rain began to pour. Over the course of the next 24 hours some 9 inches (well over 200 mm) fell, something like 250 times the expected rainfall for that time of year. As it made its way across the land, the water carried fallen trees, heavy rocks and boulders with it. Some of these created temporary dams, but when the volume of water continued to grow and broke through these ad-hoc defences, the carnage was all the greater. Lynmouth, which sits in a gorge, bore the brunt of the brutal onslaught. As one eyewitness put it: '. . . the waters rose rapidly . . . it was just like an avalanche coming through our hotel, bringing down boulders from the hills and breaking down walls, doors and windows.'

It is estimated that 90 million tonnes of water flowed through the town. Over the course of the night, 34 people died in Lynmouth (three Scouts camping on the riverbank at nearby Filleigh also perished) and hundreds more lost their homes. Cars were swept out to sea as if they were so much flotsam and jetsam, most of the area's 30 or more bridges collapsed, and a lighthouse gave way the following day. One woman who lost six members of her family described the gruesome process of identifying her grandmother's body: 'Mum identified her by this huge wart on her back because she hadn't got no head, or arms, or legs when they found her.'

It was not, however, the first time that this picturesque village had suffered a devastating deluge. There had been similar events recorded in both 1607 and 1796. Weather experts suggested that the 1952 event originated in a low-pressure front that had formed over the Atlantic Ocean several days earlier. When combined with the particular topographical features of Exmoor plus the moisture that had already built up in the ground, the ingredients were in place for a 'perfect storm'.

However, witnesses reported several other curious features about the events of that day. Some, for instance, spoke of the smell of sulphur in the air. Others described how the rain fell with such force that it hurt people's faces. There were also allegations that aircraft had been circling the area in the hours before the disaster. Scientists, some began to whisper, had been carrying out experiments aimed at influencing the weather. Had Lynmouth suffered the terrible, unforeseen consequences of their work?

It is now known that, between 1949 and 1952, the British government did indeed operate Project Cumulus, a programme set up to investigate the possibilities of weather manipulation in the hope of gaining military advantage. One of their chief avenues of investigation, it is thought, was cloud seeding, in which substances are released into the air with the aim of affecting how much moisture falls from clouds. Yet, the Ministry of Defence has never released full details of exactly what was done in the name of Project Cumulus.

Tony Speller, formerly an MP for North Devon, studied the official files but concluded that certain vital documents were missing. Meanwhile, the BBC gathered testimony from some of those involved in the experiments. One pilot, for instance, described flying over the county of Bedfordshire spraying salt to increase rainfall. There is speculation that silver iodide was also used to the same end. The theory was that very cold clouds could be targeted with specific substances to bring them under freezing point, resulting in sudden and extensive rainfall. The defence forces hoped they could use the technique, for instance, to obstruct enemy movements or to clear fog from airfields.

There is no conclusive proof that the tragedy at Lynmouth was a direct result of weather-changing experiments. We do know, however, that Project Cumulus was halted after the disaster, and that the Meteorological Office subsequently denied that any such experiments were conducted prior to 1955. Today, the science has moved on and many countries utilize certain weather-modification techniques. But back in the 1950s the technical know-how was far more rudimentary. Was there a rush to deny the existence of such work because the powers-that-be feared revelations of the damage it had wrought?

6 STARLITE

It seemed to be one of those wonderful stories of the little guy triumphing against the odds. A former hairdresser called Maurice Ward invented a heat-resistant coating that promised to revolutionize modern life. Yet in 2011 he died with his invention, 'Starlite', seemingly yet to have made any serious impact. Has the world been deprived of the greatest discovery of the 20th century?

A hairstylist skilled in mixing dyes and other beauty products, Ward entered the plastics business in the early 1980s. In 1985, moved by the tragic story of an aeroplane at Manchester Airport that caught fire on the runway, killing over 50 people in less than a minute, he set about creating a slow-burning plastic coating. After experimenting with batch after batch of ingredients blended in a food mixer, he hit upon a formula to produce plastic sheets that apparently displayed exceptional heat resistance.

Ward knew that he had found something valuable, and fiercely guarded access to the material, which his granddaughter named Starlite. He did not patent it so as not to have to reveal its composition, and while he allowed potential buyers – mostly defence organizations and commercial chemical companies – to test samples, he forbade their retention for fear of reverse engineering. Starlite, it seemed, could withstand heat equivalent to 75 Hiroshima explosions –

an amateur scientist had apparently rewritten the rules of thermodynamics.

He imagined Starlite being used in everything from fire-resistant clothing and fire doors to missile nose cones and rocket launch pads. Some of the biggest names in the field showed interest, from the UK Atomic Weapons Establishment and NASA to ICI and British Aerospace. In 1993, the public was introduced to Starlite on the BBC science show *Tomorrow's World*. A coated egg was blow-torched, and not only did it not crack, but its yolk remained runny.

But then – nothing. Deal after deal fell through, either a result of Ward's high demands or routine corporate politics. When Ward died in 2011, Starlite's recipe was reportedly known only to members of his family. It is possible, then, that a commercial deal may yet be struck and the world will see the benefits of Ward's particular brand of genius. Or perhaps, as some people believe, Starlite was appropriated long ago by an interested party more than happy for its name to fade from the public consciousness as they reaped its commercial and technical benefits . . .

7 THE BILDERBERG GROUP

The Bilderberg Group holds an annual meeting of invited European and North American power-brokers to discuss the crucial world issues of the day. Bringing together heads of state and government with giants of commerce and leading defence contractors, its lack of transparency has long made it a focus of suspicion. Some accuse it of being a cabal plotting a new world order rooted in Western capitalist doctrine.

Named after the hotel near Arnhem in the Netherlands where it first met in 1954, the group's founders included Prince Bernhard of the Netherlands, banker David Rockefeller, Polish diplomat Józef Retinger and British politician Denis Healey. Its aim was to bring together the transatlantic great and good to reinforce the liberal, free-market philosophy of the free world.

Nothing too controversial in that, you might think. Yet in the intervening years, the mixture of A-list invitees and insistence on privacy has led many to wonder just what goes on once the doors are closed. The sense of a group with the ability to pull serious strings has been heightened, thanks to a noticeable trend of future world leaders attending near the start of their careers. Bill Clinton and Tony Blair, for instance, both went before they had secured the US presidency and the UK premiership, respectively. Talent-spotting is one thing, but some say the group giving some of these people a serious boost up the ladder – and if so, what might be expected in return?

Bilderberg itself is quite sanguine about its insistence on privacy. Bringing together between 120 and 150 leading figures (at a different venue each time), from the fields of politics, finance, industry, media and academia each year to discuss what it calls 'megatrends', the Group demands meetings operate under the Chatham House Rule. That means participants may make use of any information received or ideas expressed but are prohibited from identifying either the affiliation of the speaker or any other participants – nor must anyone be directly quoted. In addition, no reporting journalists are allowed entry, all in the interests of ensuring 'participants feel they can speak freely in an environment of trust'. As former British Chancellor of the Exchequer and Bilderberg co-founder Denis Healey put it: 'The confidentiality enabled people to speak honestly without fear of repercussions.'

Yet the sense of Bilderberg as an invisible hand guiding major geopolitical trends is supported by observations from delegates who would normally be regarded as politically moderate. For instance, there is this notorious quote from Healey: 'To say we were striving for a one-world government is exaggerated, but not wholly unfair. Those of us in Bilderberg felt we couldn't go on forever fighting one another for nothing and killing people and rendering millions homeless. So we felt that a single community throughout the world would be a good thing.' For maximum impact, he really should have been sitting in a swivel chair and stroking a white cat as he said it.

Nor is the Group's image helped by its insistence on very visible and often aggressive security. While a convocation of so many influential people requires top-level protection, there have been repeated allegations of heavy-handedness, including from journalists and peaceful protestors.

British Labour MP Michael Meacher, meanwhile, has been scathing in his criticism, calling the Group a 'cabal of the rich and powerful' that looks to consolidate and extend the grip of the markets away from the public gaze. This aura of secrecy has created an extraordinary climate in which virtually diametric conspiracy theories compete for air. Some see a plot by Western power-brokers to maintain hegemony over the developing world. Left-wingers fear an assault on civil rights and personal freedom in the interests of neo-con capitalism. Right-wingers, meanwhile, allege a liberal take-over while libertarians say it all serves to strengthen the grip of 'big government'. And then there are the usual cranks convinced it is all a Zionist conspiracy. The chances are that none of these allegations is entirely fair. However, when the great and the good of the Western world lock themselves away to reach consensus on how best to address the world's 'megatrends', there are legitimate reasons why we might wish to be allowed some insight into their conclusions

A president, a bank chairman, a private equity chief, an arms dealer and an oil exec walk into a conference room . . . It sounds like the opening line of a bad joke. That, though, is the reality created by the Bilderberg Group. To imagine that everything discussed and agreed by such a coterie is in the interest of the wider public as a whole is perhaps the biggest joke of them all.

8 STUXNET

It is increasingly clear that future wars will be fought in cyber-space, where a mouse click may be able to devastate a nation's infrastructure. Even if this frightening prospect is still some way off, governments around the globe are establishing agencies devoted to cyberwarfare. The Stuxnet worm, a computer virus that wrought havoc in Iran in 2010, was a potent example of such nascent cyber weaponry.

Stuxnet came to widespread public attention in 2010, when it was reported that Iran's nuclear infrastructure had come under attack from a computer virus. One fifth of the centrifuges crucial to the operations at the Natanz uranium-enrichment facility had been knocked out of action, potentially putting back Tehran's development of a nuclear bomb by months or even years.

Stuxnet works by infecting Windows computers, attacking a specific type of programme typically used in large industrial complexes and, critically, in nuclear installations. Some experts have speculated that the virus was intended to self-destruct once its work was done but a flaw in coding meant it spread more virulently than its creators intended. Systems as far afield as the US, India and Indonesia have all been infected, though Iran suffered by far the highest number of cases. Stuxnet may even have started its work as early as 2007.

Given that Iran seems to have been the number one target, there was immediate speculation that Israel was involved in the onslaught, possibly with the assistance of the US. In 2012, the *New York Times* went so far as to suggest that the worm was part of a government operation begun by the George W. Bush administration and carried on by Barack Obama's White House. Other journalists have stated that US and Israeli involvement is all but an open secret – for instance, in 2010 the White House's then-coordinator for Arms Control and Weapons of Mass Destruction said: 'We're glad they are having trouble with their centrifuge machine and that we – the US and its allies – are doing everything we can to make sure that we complicate matters for them.'

Yet none of this amounts to official confirmation of responsibility. Furthermore, it might be argued that neither the government in Washington nor Jerusalem would mind its enemies thinking it was forging ahead in cyber-weaponry development, even if Stuxnet was in fact someone else's creation. In April 2011, the government in Tehran itself concluded that Israel and the US were responsible, but Tehran has good reason to paint both nations as enemies at every opportunity. Meanwhile, several international relations commentators have cast doubt on whether Israel and America could overcome the differences that exist between their intelligence and military communities to perfect such a potent weapon.

There are other credible suspects too – China, for instance, is known to be highly active in cyber-weaponry research. Furthermore, it has been noted that countries affected by Stuxnet are often Asian or Eurasian producers of the materials, including oil and copper, that are essential to China's own economic progress. Certainly, Beijing may have benefitted from the fallout of many of the attacks, although that is far from confirmation of culpability. Others argue that an Iranian regional rival such as Jordan might have good reason for appreciating the work of Stuxnet. Then there is the suggestion that Iran was little more than a guinea pig or incidental victim of a programme created for a quite different prime enemy. Some observers point to the fact that many of the organizations infiltrated by the virus shared a particular Russian contractor. Was it this institution that was the real intended recipient, with its partners mere collateral damage? Or perhaps Iran's nuclear infrastructure was the perfect cover for a different sort of attack altogether. Tens of thousands of industrial and security complexes have been infected around the world. As governments prepare themselves for the new age of cyber warfare, it is perhaps not so far-fetched to think that the Stuxnet attacks were a generalized weapons test. Whoever was behind the worm may now have a much clearer idea of which countries have sound defences against such attacks and which are vulnerable – knowledge that will be invaluable in future conflicts.

Some conspiracy theorists claim to have found a reference in Stuxnet's code to 'Esther', and the date that Iran executed an alleged Israeli spy – smoking guns, they say, pointing to Israeli responsibility. But to others, these are merely clumsy attempts to incriminate an innocent party. The race for cyber supremacy is such that competing nations have as much motivation to claim responsibility as to deny it.

9 MKULTRA

The Cold War had a habit of making sensible people do the maddest things, and arguably its apotheosis was the CIA-sponsored MKUltra programme, incorporating a vast number of projects run, often unknowingly, by some of the US's leading academic institutions. Designed to investigate ways of controlling human behaviour, many of its unwitting guinea pigs paid an awful price.

In the early 1950s, US intelligence agencies were concerned that their enemies in communist China, the Soviet Union and North Korea were mastering mind-control techniques. Indeed, it was feared that US troops captured in the Korean War had been subjected to such ordeals. So in April 1953, Allen Dulles, Director of the CIA, signed off on Project MKUltra. Its head, Sidney Gottlieb, was charged with researching and developing chemical, biological and radiological materials that could be used to secretly control human behaviour.

Over the next 20 years, the CIA (sometimes working with other agencies) oversaw some 150 projects through a network of colleges and universities, hospitals, prisons and private drug companies. While a few senior figures in some of these institutions were aware of where their funding was coming from, most had no idea. The motives for developing mind-control techniques were various. Some have suggested that knowledge gained was used to sharpen methods of interrogation and torture. Others speculate that the aim was to create a truth serum, to erase memories, to brainwash captives or simply to humiliate, disable and discredit targets. A few have even alleged that intelligence bosses wanted to develop a mini-army of 'Manchurian candidates' to carry out assassinations and other covert operations on behalf of the US.

Some of MKUltra's experimental subjects were injected with drugs, others kept in isolation for prolonged periods or made to endure extremes of sensory deprivation. Large numbers suffered major physical and mental symptoms as a result. Among those administered cocktails of drugs without their permission were patients of mental institutions, prisoners, drug addicts and other vulnerable members of society. Even those who willingly put themselves forward (usually for financial reward) were not furnished with sufficient information to give informed consent.

In 1974, the *New York Times* was first to publicly report aspects of MKUltra. In response, the government established an investigative committee under Senator Frank Church as well as a commission – headed by Vice-President Nelson Rockefeller – to look into the activities of the military and the security services. In 1975, Church and Rockefeller sensationally concluded that the CIA had spent over US$20 million experimenting on subjects without their permission. Furthermore, the programme had not been confined to the US, but had continued in Canada. For many years, LSD was the favoured drug of the programme. Non-consenting recipients were systematically injected, sometimes without warning while in public so as to gauge their responses. Those observing them were frequently non-scientists, rendering much of the research useless anyway.

One army employee, Dr Frank Olson, died when he fell from a thirteenth-floor window a week after being surreptitiously given the drug in 1953. His death was recorded as suicide, though members of his family claim he was murdered because the LSD experiment had rendered him a security risk. Few doubt that, one way or another, his death was a result of MKUltra. His family subsequently received a presidential apology as well as a significant financial payout. That he was the only fatality to result from the programme seems a remote prospect. Yet our knowledge of the true extent of the programme's operations and the scale of the damage caused can only ever be partial. That is because the vast majority of the official records connected to MKUltra were destroyed in 1973 on the orders of the CIA's then-Director, Richard Helms. The little paperwork that survived did so only by chance, having been incorrectly filed.

That the US authorities should be involved in experiments on non-consenting subjects is all the more breathtaking given that America had been the driving force behind the so-called Nuremberg Code, drawn up in response to revelations about human experimentation conducted by the Nazis. Such was the desire to triumph in the Cold War, that senior figures in America's intelligence community seemingly forgot their obligation to protect the rights and well-being of their own citizens. The little concrete evidence of what went on is damning enough. As to the horrors contained in the wealth of evidence destroyed before it could be studied, we may only wonder.

10 THE GEORGIA GUIDESTONES

March 1980 saw the well-attended unveiling ceremony for what is widely referred to as the 'American Stonehenge'. Five enormous stone slabs supporting a sixth combine to form an astronomical instrument. Each is inscribed with esoteric text in a number of different languages. But the identity of the individual who commissioned the work, and who he may have worked for, have remained closely guarded secrets.

On an ordinary June day in 1979, a dapper, grey-haired gentleman going by the name of Robert C. Christian turned up at Elberton Granite Finishing in Georgia's Elbert County. Calling himself a representative of a 'small group of loyal Americans', he had a meeting with Joe Fendley, president of the company, during which he explained the very particular details of a project he wanted the firm to undertake – a set of enormous stones crafted into an astronomical instrument that would act as compass, calendar and clock.

Fendley was initially sceptical. The scale of the project was huge – each of five supporting stones was to be almost six metres (20 ft) tall, supporting a suitably massive capstone. Together they would weigh close to 110 tonnes (250,000 lb). He had never worked on anything approaching this size, but his client was able to supply detailed plans, and a meeting with Wyatt C. Martin, president of Granite City Bank, confirmed that Christian had the finances in place. Fendley took on the job, and once a plot of land was purchased, no one working on the project saw Christian again.

Each of the stones was to be engraved with a script provided by Christian, translated into eight languages (English, Spanish, Russian, Chinese, Arabic, Hebrew, Hindi and Swahili) and comprising ten directives:

1. Maintain humanity under 500,000,000 in perpetual balance with nature.
2. Guide reproduction wisely – improving fitness and diversity.
3. Unite humanity with a living new language.
4. Rule passion – faith – tradition – and all things with tempered reason.
5. Protect people and nations with fair laws and just courts.
6. Let all nations rule internally, resolving external disputes in a world court.
7. Avoid petty laws and useless officials.
8. Balance personal rights with social duties.
9. Prize truth – beauty – love – seeking harmony with the infinite.
10. Be not a cancer on the Earth – Leave room for nature – Leave room for nature.

Interpretations of the wording vary wildly. Some consider it nothing more than harmless, New Age gobbledygook. A few see the assertion of a valuable and liberal agenda, underpinned by fairness and justice. Others, though, detect something more sinister – even fascistic – in the call for a curb on population, the focus on ordered reproduction and the assertion of a new global language. Engraved on the capstone in Egyptian

hieroglyphs, classical Greek, Sanskrit and Babylonian cunei-
form is the phrase: 'Let these be guidestones to an Age of
Reason.' It would seem the authors have laid out nothing less
than instructions for reinventing a post-apocalyptic society.

But only those behind the construction of the stones truly
know what it all means. Central to unpicking their secrets
is the identity of R.C. Christian, but he seems unlikely to be
found anytime soon: he freely admitted that he was using a
pseudonym, that the project had been 20 years in the making,
and that on-going anonymity was essential. Christian's business dealings were conducted from disparate corners of the
US so that even establishing where he might be based was
impossible. Bank president Wyatt Martin, the only person
known to have been privy to his true identity, burned all
the paperwork in his possession in 2012, determined to take
Christian's secret to the grave.

So we are left with speculation. There are some convinced
the guidestones are the work of a sinister group looking to
establish a New World Order. Some point to the Rosicrucians,
a secret holy order that emerged in Germany in the late Middle
Ages. According to their ancient manifesto, 'The word R.C.
should be their seal, mark and character.' Clearly, they argue,
R.C. Christian was playing on this reference. Another theory
is that the colossal structure is intended as a landing post for
alien invaders sometime in the future. More mundanely, a
few have accused Joe Fendley of devising an enormous publicity stunt. Whatever the truth, it is perhaps the words of Mr
Martin that should resonate most. He said of R.C. Christian:
'All along, he said that who he was and where he came from
had to be kept a secret. He said mysteries work that way. If
you want to keep people interested, you can let them know
only so much.'

11 THE MAJESTIC 12

In the mid-1980s a series of astonishing documents, apparently leaked from the US government, was made public. They seemingly contained devastating evidence of a secret committee appointed by the US President to manage and investigate alleged UFO landings and contacts with extraterrestrial life. Most commentators now accept that the documents are an elaborate hoax – but who was behind it and why?

I t was 1984 when a leaked eight-page file started doing the rounds of the UFOlogy community. It claimed to reveal how US President Harry Truman had instigated 'Operation Majestic 12', setting up a 12-man committee in the aftermath of a supposed UFO crash-landing at Roswell, New Mexico, in 1947. This gang of 12 was to work undercover, exploring ways to cover up the 'Roswell Incident' while simultaneously exploiting the associated technology that had come into American hands. In addition, it was to discuss how to manage future extraterrestrial engagement.

A year after the file came to light, a team of UFO investigators were anonymously directed to a 'declassified' memo in the National Archives, supposedly sent from a general to a senior White House official during President Eisenhower's tenure. It contained an ostensibly corroborating reference to Majestic 12. By the mid-1990s, a Majestic 12 handbook was also in circulation. However, the FBI, among others, concluded that all of this documentation was bogus.

While a few hard-line conspiracy theorists remain convinced that Majestic 12 was an all-too-real entity that carried out its work ruthlessly, and even killed when it was deemed necessary, the broad consensus among the UFOlogical community is that the whole thing was a complex and far-reaching hoax. Key to this belief is evidence from former US Air Force Officer of Special Investigations Richard Doty (see page 168), who claimed Majestic 12 was deliberately created to disseminate misinformation.

But why would US authorities go to such lengths to discredit a community that many believe is full of cranks anyway? A counter-theory is that they developed such schemes in the hope of gradually preparing the public for the revelation that we really are not the only world to support life. Meanwhile others, with their feet planted firmly on this planet, suggest that such a campaign of misinformation can only be aimed at diverting attention from darker truths nearer to home that the powers-that-be may not want to come to light.

12 THE BLACK SOX SCANDAL

The revelation that a large contingent of the Chicago White Sox baseball team had taken pay-offs to throw the 1919 World Series was a scandal that pierced the very heart of America. The implication of beloved and supremely talented hitter 'Shoeless' Joe Jackson only made matters worse. To this day, he is barred from entry into the sport's Hall of Fame – but was Shoeless Joe the victim of a grave injustice?

'Shoeless' Joe was a folk hero until 1920, when allegations surfaced that he and seven fellow White Sox players had conspired to fix the previous year's World Series. The general sense of disbelief was captured in a (probably apocryphal) encounter following Jackson's appearance before a grand jury. A small boy is said to have pleaded, 'Say it ain't so, Joe,' to which he either did not reply, or else said, 'Yes, kid, I'm afraid it is.'

The scam was organized by a gambling cabal that offered key players large amounts of money – considerably more than a year's salary in most cases. Although all eight were acquitted of criminal charges in September 1920, the sport's governing authorities dispensed lifetime bans. There is little doubt that the other players did indeed manipulate their performances to ensure particular results, but defenders of Jackson point to his record in the games – he ended with a Series-record batting average, a run-out and no errors to his name. Surely he played too well for someone trying to lose?

Yet few dispute that Jackson knew of the conspiracy. He is said to have refused a large sum of money on at least two occasions, and unsuccessfully attempted to meet with White Sox boss Charles Comiskey to reveal the scandal. Other witnesses testified that he even asked Comiskey to bench him for the World Series so as not to be involved. Although he subsequently admitted to a role in the scandal, the debate continues as to whether Jackson was merely guilty of not stopping the fix, rather than of actively participating. He certainly received money, but reputedly only when it was effectively forced on him after initial refusals. The other conspirators even confirmed that he had been absent from meetings arranging the fix, admitting they brought Jackson's name into the affair merely to leverage credibility with the gambling ring.

So Jackson, a simple sort of guy, may be one of sport's saddest patsies. In 1949, he told *SPORT Magazine*: 'I can say that my conscience is clear, and that I'll stand on my record in that World Series.'

13 THE KATYN FOREST MASSACRE

In 1990, amid the collapse of the Soviet Union, the Kremlin admitted responsibility for a war crime it had previously attempted to blame on the Nazis. In April and May 1940, Stalin's secret police killed some 22,000 members of the Polish Officer Corps and other Polish prisoners, most of them in the Katyn Forest in the west of Russia. But were Washington and London complicit in the cover-up?

Stalin ordered the systematic execution of Poland's military and intellectual elite in the belief that Polish resolve against Russian hegemony would be broken. It was a campaign of terror carried out under the shadow of the 1939 German-Soviet non-aggression pact, which saw Poland invaded by both powers.

Yet by 1941, Hitler and Stalin were at war and Poland was under sole German occupation. When, in 1943, the Berlin government announced the discovery of the Katyn graves, the Polish government-in-exile in London called for an International Red Cross investigation. Stalin refused to cooperate, alleging that the victims were killed by Nazi forces in 1941. It was a line that Moscow held until 1990, but there is significant evidence that points to the administrations in both London and Washington knowing the truth long before then. Yet neither government felt able or compelled to condemn its erstwhile wartime ally.

Shortly after the Nazi reports emerged, Churchill reputedly told a senior Polish military figure: 'Alas, the German revelations are probably true. The Bolsheviks can be very cruel.' Furthermore, in 1943, Nazi personnel took Allied prisoners of war to view the bodies. Most were convinced the crime was indeed committed by the USSR, and sent coded messages to Washington to that end, only for the information to be suppressed at the highest levels of government. There is also a report sent to President Roosevelt by the UK's ambassador to the Polish government-in-exile, Owen O'Malley. It concludes: 'There is now available a good deal of negative evidence, the cumulative effect of which is to throw serious doubt on Russian disclaimers of responsibility for the massacre.'

Roosevelt and Churchill were both wary of Stalin, but equally knew their fortunes were tied to his. Yet even as war demands that leaders show ruthless pragmatism, it is a stain upon all those involved that the truth of the Katyn Forest massacre was subject to such an international conspiracy of silence.

14 THE ISABELLA STEWART GARDNER MUSEUM THEFTS

It was arguably the most audacious art heist in history, involving the theft of 13 works of art from the prestigious Isabella Stewart Gardner Museum in Boston. The thieves made off with pictures by such legendary names as Rembrandt, Vermeer, Degas and Manet, conservatively valued at US$500 million. And a quarter of a century later, none of the pilfered works has been recovered.

The crime was executed by two men disguised as Boston police officers. They told a guard that they were responding to a call, and he dutifully granted them entry, whereupon the assailants tied him up with one of his colleagues. By the time the alarm was raised the following morning, the robbers had casually removed works from a number of rooms. Such is the fame of several of the pieces (including Rembrandt's 'Storm on the Sea of Galilee') that it would be impossible to sell them on the open market. Furthermore, the way the thieves made their way from floor to floor suggests this was perhaps theft to order, undertaken for some Blofeld-like supervillain with a private gallery.

The FBI's efforts to recover the masterpieces have so far met with failure. There is strong reason to believe that the plundered art has travelled extensively around Massachusetts, Connecticut and Philadelphia but, despite confirmed sightings of at least some of the works in the early 2000s, the trail has gone cold again.

In 2013, the Gardner Museum and the FBI jointly offered a US$5 million reward for the art's safe return. With the statute of limitations for the original theft having expired, it was also suggested that anyone who subsequently handled the stolen property might receive immunity from prosecution in return for their cooperation. Yet the appeal yielded nothing. Instead, the best tip-off to date came in 2010, when the FBI received intelligence leading them to three men with organized crime connections. Despite this, none was charged with any felony, and by 2013 only one of the three was still alive (and still vehemently denying involvement). Meanwhile, the location of the works remains as elusive as ever.

It is clear that there are career criminals who know precisely where the Gardner hoard now resides, and it is difficult to see how they can ever hope to profit from such 'hot' property. But whether they may yet find it in their hearts to return these treasures for the rest of us to enjoy again, only time will tell.

15 LISTON vs ALI

Sonny Liston and Muhammad Ali fought each other twice. Their first bout in 1964 saw Ali (then known as Cassius Clay) sensationally defy the odds to overcome the champion Liston in the seventh round. Their rematch a year later lasted less than a round, with Liston hitting the floor after apparently receiving a punch that millions of fans believe never connected. Did Liston, as many have claimed, throw the fight?

'Fight of the century' is a much over-used phrase, but the second Liston vs Ali bout had a legitimate claim to the title. On 25 May 1965 in Lewiston, Maine, the two boxers clashed for the second time. Clay, by now called Muhammad Ali, was well on his way towards greatness, but only a fool discounted Liston's threat.

And yet, about halfway through Round One, Liston hit the canvas like a sack of potatoes. The referee counted him out and a vast live and television audience was left feeling strangely cheated. Their chief complaint was that it did not look as if Ali had caught Liston with a punch of any power. And so began the legend of the so-called 'phantom punch'.

Many simply believed Liston had taken a dive. The famous sports writer Jimmy Cannon said that Ali's strike 'couldn't have crushed a grape', although other commentators spoke instead of a devastating assault of 'amazing speed'. Rumours that he had thrown the fight nonetheless plagued Liston right up until his apparent suicide in 1971.

If he did dive, of course, it is possible that somebody paid him enough to make it worth his while. Alternatively, there are suggestions that Liston was in debt to some serious underworld figures – was the fight his way of paying them off? Another intriguing explanation rests with Ali's religious and political activism. He had recently converted to Islam and joined the Black Muslims group headed by Elijah Muhammad. This had offended the famed black civil rights campaigner Malcolm X, whose people are said to have wanted to extract some form of revenge. Did Elijah's people counter by getting to Sonny (perhaps via his family) in a bid to ensure that their man was guaranteed the win? Stranger things have happened, especially in boxing.

And in 2014, declassified documents revealed that the FBI suspected the original fight had also been fixed. In 1966, in memos to FBI Director J. Edgar Hoover, mob-connected Las Vegas gambler Ash Renick was accused of arranging the result. Ali–Liston: a legendary rivalry where everything was not as it seemed?

16 THE IRISH CROWN JEWELS

The Order of St Patrick was established by King George III of England and Ireland in the late 18th century. Its ornate insignia came to be known as the Irish Crown Jewels. Moved to Dublin Castle for safekeeping in 1903, the jewels went missing four years later, never to be returned. Was the culprit known to the authorities but protected in order to avert a scandal?

The Irish regalia comprised a star and badge decorated with almost 400 precious stones, including diamonds, rubies and emeralds. They were under the protection of the Ulster King of Arms, and in 1903 were placed in a specially designed safe to be kept in a strongroom at Dublin Castle. Alas, the safe proved too large to get through the doorway, and so instead it was put in the office of the King of Arms, Arthur Vicars. While several individuals possessed keys to this room, Vicars alone held keys for the safe.

Yet sometime between 11 June and 6 July 1907, the regalia went missing. Before long Scotland Yard's Detective Chief Inspector John Kane was brought in to assist the Dublin police investigation. Today, rumours persist that he authored a report which named the thief, only for it to be supressed by his Irish counterparts. Meanwhile, a specially convened commission failed to finger the culprit but did accuse Vicars of not exercising 'due vigilance or proper care as the custodian of the regalia'.

Allegations flew around. Some accused nationalist criminals, while others suspected a Unionist plot (possibly to embarrass the Liberal government of the day). One theory had Vicars falling foul of a comely con woman, while he in turn accused his deputy, Francis Shackleton.

Shackleton was the younger brother of legendary Polar explorer Ernest, but was decidedly the black sheep of the family. Years later, he would be convicted of fraud and forced to live out the rest of his life under an assumed name. According to a 1908 article published in the US, he (and possibly an accomplice) was known to be the thief, but had threatened to reveal details of unseemly behaviour at the castle if prosecuted, including homosexual relationships that would have been illegal at the time. Left as scapegoat for the affair, Vicars had little choice but to resign, though he later fought and won a libel case against the *Daily Mail*. He died an embittered man in 1921, shot by IRA insurgents. The evidence available today suggests he had good reason to feel aggrieved.

17 THE PROTOCOLS OF THE ELDERS OF ZION

The Protocols of the Elders of Zion is a late-19th/early-20th-century forgery that purports to be the minutes from a meeting of high-level Jewish leaders (the 'Elders of Zion') discussing their plans for global domination. Despite being identified as a hoax as early as 1921, the text took on a horrible life of its own, fuelling anti-Semitism first in Russia and then internationally. But who was responsible for its creation?

First published in 1903, The Protocols masqueraded as the minutes from a meeting held a few years before. It was presented as evidence of a plot to establish global Jewish hegemony by, among other things, subverting the morality of non-Jews and leveraging control of the world's banks and media. Echoing long-held anti-Semitic myths, it appeared in a number of Russian editions over the following three years.

At the time, there was a movement keen to blame the Jews for Russia's military humiliation by Japan in 1905, and for the ills deriving from the ensuing revolution. Some believe the book was circulated in the hope of persuading Tsar Nicholas II that his concessions to modernizers were fuelling a Jewish global takeover. Following the October Revolution of 1917, the text was brought to the West by fleeing 'White Russians' intent on identifying the Jews with

Lenin's victorious Bolsheviks. It found a receptive readership in much of Europe, and also in the United States, where automobile magnate Henry Ford personally stumped up the money for a print run of 500,000 copies.

However, as early as 1921 there was strong evidence that the document was a hoax. Catherine Radziwill, a Polish-Lithuanian princess, told an audience in New York that she had been shown the manuscript back in 1905 and knew it to be authored by two Russian journalists at the behest of a senior member of the Russian security services. Even if she was not considered the most reliable of witnesses, her testimony was soon backed up by an exposé in the venerable *Times* newspaper. This revealed that much of the content of The Protocols was plagiarized from an 1864 French work by Maurice Joly attacking the rule of Napoleon III. Depicting a dialogue in Hell between Machiavelli and Montesquieu, the work was plundered by The Protocols' author(s), who took Machiavelli's words and represented them as the opinions of the Elders of Zion. Later studies showed that other parts of the text were lifted from *Biarritz*, an 1868 novel by German author Hermann Goedsche.

Yet despite the overwhelming evidence of fakery, The Protocols continued to attract readers including Adolf Hitler himself, who cited the work as justification for his anti-Jewish policies. Perversely believing that the denials were proof of its authenticity (based on the argument 'They would say that, wouldn't they?'), Hitler wrote in his ranting political manifesto *Mein Kampf*: '. . . with positively terrifying certainty they reveal the nature and activity of the Jewish people and expose their inner contexts as well as their ultimate final aims.' Today, the text continues to be sold in some parts of the world as a genuine historical document.

But in recent years, the opening up of archives in post-communist Russia seems to have confirmed the identity of one of the text's primary authors. His name was Mathieu Golovinski, a Russian-born aristocrat with strong ties to France. A political activist and writer, he was at one time a tsarist supporter before throwing his weight behind the Bolshevik communists. Partly as a result of happenstance, he fell into espionage and was seemingly commissioned to write The Protocols around the turn of the twentieth century by Pyotr Rachkovsky, who headed the Paris office of Russia's intelligence service. Golovinsky also knew Charles Joly, son of Maurice Joly, when both were employed in the French capital – Princess Catherine, it seems, was right all along.

Yet even if the question of principal authorship seems to have been cleared up, it is not so easy to assume that The Protocols were the brainchild of Rachkovsky on his own. How far up the chain of command did the order to produce the fraudulent work originate? And what other powerful figures in Russian society were complicit in establishing the hateful work as genuine? Given how widely it was promoted and took hold, the suspicion must be that the text was the product of an extensive and formidable conspiracy.

Perhaps the darkest aspect of the whole story is that despite overwhelming evidence that it was created specifically to fool, there remain those who cite it in support of their own political agendas. What may have begun as a fiendish ruse designed to encourage the forlorn Tsar Nicholas II to take a hard line against perceived domestic opponents in early 20th-century Russia evolved into a tool that has been used to justify terrible crimes against Jews for a century or more.

MYSTERY MESSAGES

18 THE VOYNICH MANUSCRIPT

In the library of Yale University in Connecticut lies one of the most intriguing books on the planet. Called the Voynich Manuscript after the Polish rare book dealer who rediscovered it in the early 20th century, the volume consists of an encrypted text that no one can yet translate, along with striking esoteric illustrations. Some see it as a fantastical hoax, while others hope it may eventually reveal some great wisdom.

The manuscript, a little smaller than A5 in area and about 5 cm (2 inches) thick, consists of some 240 vellum (calf-skin) pages, covered in handwritten text in a language of unknown origin. Most pages also contain a liberal scattering of idiosyncratic illustrations and diagrams. Carbon dating suggests it was created some time in the first four decades of the 15th century. Based on the nature of the illustrations, it is believed the text may have been divided into five principle sections: biology, astrology, pharmacy, herbs and recipes.

Tracking the manuscript's ownership is a feat in itself. When Voynich turned it up in Italy in 1912, he found within its leaves a letter stating that the Holy Roman Emperor Rudolf II (1552–1612), had once bought it for 600 ducats (about US$100,000 today). It later came into the possession of Georg Baresch, an alchemist active in Prague in the early 17th century. In 1666, Baresch brought it to the attention of

Athanasius Kircher, a Jesuit scholar with a reputation for deciphering ancient languages.

Kircher wanted to buy it but Baresch refused to sell. Instead, on Baresch's death it passed to the dead man's friend, Johannes Marcus Marci, rector of Charles University in Prague. He in turn handed it over to Kircher for inspection. The trail then goes cold until Wilfred Voynich picked it up in a job lot of works sold off by the Collegio Romano in Italy. Following his death in 1930, it went through several more hands until it was finally donated to Yale in 1969.

It is broadly agreed that the text contains around 170,000 individual symbols, although some are rendered indistinctly so the precise number is uncertain. Linguists suggest the 'language' is composed from an alphabet of between 20 and 30 major symbols. Many of the world's leading cryptographers, including notable code-breakers of the First and Second World Wars, have devoted years of their lives to trying to crack the code but so far to no avail.

Because of this singular lack of progress, some are now convinced that there is nothing to be cracked. That is to say, they believe the language used is gobbledegook, and that the manuscript was created as a piece of mischief designed to trick somebody into believing that within its apparent code lay great secrets. Whether this was done with financial profit in mind or simply for the joy of playing a trick is disputed.

Among the most regularly suggested authors is 14th-century Franciscan friar and philosopher Roger Bacon, although his dates and those of the manuscript do not match well. The case has also been made for authorship by another great polymath, Leonardo da Vinci. Meanwhile, John Dee (infamous Elizabethan mathematician and astrologer) and Edward Kelley (wannabe alchemist and sometime partner-in-crime of Dee) are seen as the most likely culprits to have sold the manuscript to Rudolf – with some going so far as to claim that one or both of them forged it in order to extract riches from the Emperor.

Yet if the manuscript is a hoax, its creator went above and beyond the call of duty. In an age when relatively un-sophisticated forgeries could pass muster in the courts of Europe, why go to all the time, effort and expense of creat-ing a work that continues to confound experts into the 21st century? Yet in 2003 Gordon Rugg, a computer scientist at Keele University in the UK, devised a programme based on a 16th-century encryption device that he claimed could have helped produce the nonsensical text in little over three months. Suddenly, Edward Kelley re-emerged as a prime suspect.

Nevertheless, the suspicion lingers that the text and its myriad intricate illustrations are far too complex to be a hoax. Several leading linguists using statistical analysis have detected a pattern in the symbols akin to known languages. Whether the symbols represent an entirely new language or an encoded existing one is moot, but it all tends against the idea that the text is random and meaningless. So the quest for the truth will go on, and is perhaps what truly gives the manuscript its magic. We can at least be sure that its author(s) defiantly took the solution to the mystery to their grave.

19 THE LOST LITERATURE OF THE MAYA

The decline of the Maya culture represents one of the great historical mysteries. Why did one of the world's leading civilizations prosper for 2,500 years and then, apparently suddenly, collapse? Sadly, our knowledge of the Maya is greatly reduced as a result of one of the most terrible acts of cultural vandalism ever recorded – precisely what Diego de Landa's 'bonfire of the vanities' cost us is unlikely ever to be known.

It is a puzzle that has intrigued historians, archaeologists and anthropologists for centuries: what brought the great Central American Maya civilization to its knees between the 8th and 10th centuries? War or civil strife? Disease? Natural disaster? Overhunting? Alien invasion? No idea was considered too absurd for consideration. Today, the consensus is that the Maya were brought down by prolonged drought exacerbated by overeager deforestation.

Whatever prompted the decline, the Maya fled their cities in droves, never to return. By the time Spanish conquistadors arrived in the 16th century, descendants were scattered across an area including modern Belize, El Salvador, Guatemala, Honduras and Mexico. Elements of Maya culture lived on through them, as well as through a plethora of texts and monuments inscribed in the complex glyphs of the Maya language. The Maya were sophisticated scientists, mathematicians and architects, and their culture embraced a rich spiritualism. All in all, these ancients had much wisdom to bequeath to the modern world. However, among the Spanish settlers of the time was one Friar Diego de Landa, Bishop of Yucatán, who was on a strange spiritual mission of his own.

On the one hand, de Landa provided arguably the definitive ethnological study of the Maya in his work *Relación de las cosas de Yucatán* (*On the Things of Yucatán*). On the other, charged with Catholic zeal and appalled by the apparent Maya predilection for human sacrifice, on 12 July 1562 he orchestrated a mass burning of books and idolatrous imagery. He claimed 27 texts went up in smoke but others said it was a hundred times as many. Whatever the precise number, he wiped out almost the entire record of the language save for four codices that survived the conflagration.

Since the 19th century, Maya language has been largely deciphered via the study of the texts that survived de Landa's attack, alongside later archaeological finds. However, what the Bishop sent up in flames is lost to us forever.

20 THE KRYPTOS CODE

In the grounds of the US Central Intelligence Agency at Langley, Virginia, stands a sculpture called 'Kryptos'. Designed by Jim Sanborn, it is adorned with four coded messages, each fiendishly difficult to break. Three have been decoded, but the fourth code is yet to be mastered – a significant achievement, given that it is viewed by many of the world's pre-eminent intelligence experts on a daily basis.

Sanborn designed 'Kryptos' (meaning 'hidden' in Greek) in conjunction with former CIA cryptologist Ed Sheidt, after winning a competition for the $250,000 commission. Central to its design are four large, curved copper panels: each contains an individual code, made up from the 26 letters of the Latin alphabet along with a number of question marks.

Sanborn has admitted the fourth code is the hardest to crack, but expected the first three to be broken within weeks. In fact, they were solved only years after the sculpture's November 1990 dedication. In 1999, a Californian computer scientist broke cover to say he had untangled the code but the CIA reported that one of their men had achieved the same a year earlier. However, it eventually emerged that the glory belonged to the National Security Agency, where a team had come up with a solution way back in June 1993.

The first code was a poetic flourish composed by Sanborn, the second referred to an object hidden in the grounds at Langley (the location of which was known to former CIA Director William Webster), while the third referenced Howard Carter's account of discovering Tutankhamun's tomb in 1922. The contents of the fourth, comprising 97 symbols, remain a mystery – and one not made easier to solve by a number of deliberate and accidental typographical errors.

Armies of professional and amateur cryptologists continue to work on the conundrum, and Sanborn has set up an official website where possible solutions can be verified (or more commonly not). In 2010, he even provided a clue in the hope of moving things along. With Kryptos's 20th anniversary approaching, he revealed that a section comprising the letters 'nypvtt' should be decoded as 'Berlin'.

But for now, the code continues to confound. 'I think it would be great if it retains its mystery,' Sanborn has said. 'I will probably give out some other clues in ten more years, and if I'm still around, ten more years after that.'

21 THE SHUGBOROUGH INSCRIPTION

The stone and marble folly known as the Shepherd's Monument stands in the grounds of the Shugborough Estate in Staffordshire, England. At its base is an inscription of eight letters – O U O S V A V V – bookended by a D and an M at a slightly lower level. Is it a message intended for the members of a notorious secret society? Whatever the intent, its meaning has confounded some of the most brilliant cryptologists.

The 365-hectare (900-acre) Shugborough Estate is the ancestral home of the Lords of Lichfield. It came into the possession of the Anson family in the 1620s and was considerably extended in the 1740s. Though the work was commissioned by Thomas Anson, it was largely funded by his brother George, who had accumulated a fortune as one of the country's most successful admirals.

The Shepherd's Monument was erected in the period 1748–63 and carved by Peter Scheemakers, a celebrated Flemish sculptor. Above the mysterious array of letters, the monument is adorned with a carved relief based on a picture by baroque master Nicolas Poussin called 'Les Bergers d'Arcadie' ('The Shepherds of Arcadia'). Poussin's original resides in the Louvre in Paris and depicts a female figure and three shepherds by a tomb, pointing to an inscription that reads 'Et in Arcadia ego' ('And I am in Arcadia too').

But what of the sequence of letters inscribed underneath? The D at the beginning and M at the end echo the use of those two letters on Roman tombs. In that context they serve as an acronym for the phrase 'Diis Manibus', which roughly translates as 'For the spirit-gods'. Among those who became captivated by the mystery behind the remaining eight letters were notables including the potter Josiah Wedgwood, Charles Dickens and Charles Darwin. None, though, could satisfactorily explain what it meant.

One of the most popular theories is that the code relates to a secret kept by the Priory of Sion, an alleged sect that some consider a successor organization to the Knight's Templar. The Priory of Sion, it has been suggested (by, among others, *Da Vinci Code* author Dan Brown) are guardians of priceless religious relics including the Holy Grail, and protect vital knowledge about the true nature of Jesus Christ. Over the years Poussin has been proposed as a leading member of the Priory, prompting speculation that the adaptation of one of his key works on the Shugborough monument is no mere chance. On the contrary, the argument goes, it is key to unlocking the mystery of the encryption underneath.

But if the inscription points the way to the Holy Grail or some other secret, no one has yet been able to decipher its precise instructions. One anonymous American with an apparent military background used a complex grid-based decryption technique to come up with the phrase: 'Jesus H Defy'. The H, he argued, represented the Greek letter 'chi' (used to denote Christ), and he interpreted the message as suggesting that Christ was an earthly prophet, not a divine being. Was this the sentiment intended to be shared by the Priory of Sion's fraternity? While the anonymous code-breaker undoubtedly had well-honed skills, it takes several leaps of faith to conclude that he definitively cracked the puzzle.

In the mid-2000s, a team of veteran cryptologists who had helped break the notoriously difficult German Enigma code during the Second World War were let loose on the Shugborough mystery – but even they were equivocal when offering up possible solutions. One of them, Sheila Lawn, echoed a theory first put forward in the 1950s that the letters most likely stand for a Latin verse: 'Optima Uxoris Optima Sororis Viduus Amantissimus Vovit Virtutibus', which translates as 'Best Wife, Best Sister, Widower Most Loving Vows Virtuously': so is the inscription simply a dedication from George Anson to his dead wife? Sheila's husband and fellow Bletchley Park veteran, Oliver, on the other hand, suggested that the Priory of Sion interpretation might have legs after all.

With a little lateral thinking, others have concluded the letters are an acrostic for a specific Bible verse or piece of classical poetry. One dedicated mystery-solver, A.J. Morton, believes the letters were inscribed only in the 19th century and are nothing more than the initials of later generations of the extended Anson family. Meanwhile, author Peter Oberg has claimed that they relate to the the Oak Island Money Pit, site of a purported treasure off the coast of Nova Scotia.

Antique graffiti, love poetry, directions to an ancient relic or evidence of a religious secret – the truth behind the inscription remains as elusive as it ever was. As Richard Kemp, Shugborough's general manager, put it: 'They could of course be a family secret, which everyone in the family knows about and which is of little consequence. But it's like Everest, you climb it because it's there. There's a code here, so everyone wants to unravel it.'

22 ROSSLYN CHAPEL

The Collegiate Chapel of St Matthew the Apostle at Rosslyn, in Scotland's Esk Valley, is a Medieval masterpiece immersed in mystery. Much speculation focuses on the idiosyncratic carvings that adorn its interiors, whose meanings are tantalizingly elusive. Claims include links to Freemasonry and the Knights Templar, while Dan Brown's *Da Vinci Code* suggested that it holds the key to the Holy Grail legend.

Established in 1446 by William St Clair, Earl of Caithness, Rosslyn Chapel was not completed until the 1480s. When finished, it contained many examples of bravura stonemasonry. For instance, the extraordinary Prentice Pillar was – so the story goes – carved by a humble apprentice who was slaughtered by his master in a fit of professional jealousy when he saw how grand it was. There are some 120 bearded green men carved into the walls of the church, along with 213 cubes around the ceiling, each engraved with one of 12 mysterious symbols. Are these features, as some believe, purveyors of great lost secrets?

Suggestions that the carvings represent either a Templar or Masonic code are largely undermined by the fact that the chapel did not come into being until 130 years after the dissolution of the former and a couple of centuries before any documented mention of the latter. Given the shakiness of those connections, it is also easy to dismiss speculation that the carvings encrypt any Grail revelations.

However, that does not mean that the ornate stonework isn't communicating some different but equally fascinating message. The green men, for instance, have associations with paganism, while the Prentice Pillar is adorned with a decidedly non-Biblical dragon. Was William St Clair expressing a complex belief system that encompassed more than his ostensibly Catholic faith? Some see the church as an allegorical story in physical form, with the green men serving as principle motifs. Starting at the east of the church and working round, the figures get progressively older. In the east of the church, the iconography deals with new life, the spring season and so on. By the time you reach the north of the chapel, the green men are old and the theme is death. The church, according to this interpretation, tells the progressive tale of life itself.

Other commentators believe the carvings are most interesting in the way they undermine accepted historical narratives. Specifically, it has been suggested that the chapel contains images of, among other things, Indian sweetcorn and American cacti – plants from a New World that Columbus did not reach until 1492, at least a decade after the church was completed. How did the chapel's architects have prior knowledge of these American plants? Some are certain they did not, arguing that the images are in fact variants on common Medieval artistic symbols. Others, however, suggest the church was a font of rare and exotic knowledge.

Perhaps most intriguing of all are the cubes on the ceiling. One particularly enticing theory was developed by the father-and-son team of Thomas and Stuart Mitchell.

Over many years around the turn of the millennium, they honed their interpretation of the cubes as a musical score. Each of the cubes' 12 enigmatic symbols, they said, represents a Chladni pattern. These are patterns, first observed in the 18th century by Ernst Chladni, produced by powder on a metal plate when it is vibrated by a sustained musical note. For instance, A below middle C produces a rhombus-type shape, while other notes produce hexagons, diamonds and flowers. All of these symbols can be found on the cubes, raising the question of whether Rosslyn's architects were aware of the Chladni patterns centuries before Chladni himelf was born.

After his father hit upon the potential code, Stuart Mitchell orchestrated a score that has since been performed at the chapel. Intriguingly, it contains a chord progression known as the Devil's Interval, once banned by the Catholic Church for its diabolical sound. Was this St Clair having another quiet dig at the Roman Catholic Church? Mitchell Jr, meanwhile, even speculated that the music might have been composed with the expectation that its acoustics would precipitate a physical manifestation in the chapel – such as, in his own words, 'something falling loose . . . like a safe'. Although this has not been witnessed, there is evidence that some of the cubes were replaced in the past in the incorrect order – so perhaps the necessary music has not yet been reproduced.

Whether you are convinced that the chapel's engravings signpost the way to the Holy Grail, tell the tale of life itself or do something else entirely, Rosslyn's carvings hold an enduring fascination. It is only accentuated by the fact that no one alive today can say for sure what their creators truly intended.

23 THE EASTER ISLAND GLYPHS

Easter Island in the Pacific Ocean is a true land of mystery, most famous for its 900 or so giant stone figures carved between about AD 1100 and 1700. But equally mystifying are a series of carved wooden tablets, inscribed in what is believed to be the lost script of rongorongo. Confounding the best efforts of modern linguists to decipher them, what secrets might these texts hold?

The Rapa Nui are the indigenous people of Easter Island, and rongorongo the written form of their native tongue. European visitors in the 19th century recorded the existence of many wooden artefacts carved with symbols ranging from geometric shapes to renderings of humans, plants and animals. Many linguists believe these glyphs represent a form of writing of enormous interest – with no evidence of historical written language on neighbouring islands, it would seem to have developed independent of other linguistic influences – a great rarity in human history.

There is much debate as to how old the language might be. Many academics believe it may only have developed after Spain claimed the island in 1770. Regardless, by the end of the following century rongorongo was a dead, indecipherable script. This sad demise seems to have resulted from a mixture of foreign cultural imperialism and a desire by the

Rapa Nui people to preserve the secrets of their heritage. The local population was decimated in the 19th century by the introduction of Western diseases and attacks from Peruvian slave traders. Furthermore, missionaries fearful that the Rapa Nui language was rooted in pagan traditions suppressed it and destroyed items adorned with rongorongo inscriptions. When Father Joseph Eyraud set out to record the language in the 1860s, he found nobody able to translate the extant texts.

Either the knowledge was entirely lost, or the Rapa Nui were unwilling to help someone whose predecessors had treated their culture so ruthlessly. By the late 1870s, the island's indigenous population was reduced to little more than a hundred – all those able to read rongorongo were either dead or had been deported. Today, only 25 wooden tablets inscribed with the glyphs are known to survive and none reside on Easter Island. It is possible that rongorongo has much to tell us not only about the people of Easter Island but about the formation of language itself. Unfortunately, the cultural insensitivities of a previous age have left us in the dark.

24 THE SEGO CANYON PETROGLYPHS

The spectacular sandstone cliffs of Sego Canyon in the US state of Utah record the cultural and spiritual lives of Native American peoples over some 8,000 years. Carved and painted artworks fall into three major groups, the oldest of which, the so-called Barrier Canyon rock art, incorporate strange images that leave many visitors dumbfounded – were Mesoamerican people communing with extraterrestrials?

The most recent images found in Sego Canyon date from the period 1300–1880. Known as the Ute Indian petroglyphs (rock-carved symbols), they show human and animal figures. Next oldest are the Fremont Indian petroglyphs, created between AD 600 and 1250 and characterized by humanoid figures with outsized bodies and small heads.

In stark contrast, the Barrier Canyon images include both petroglyphs and pictographs (images painted on the rock surface). They were created by nomadic hunter-gatherers of the Archaic period – cave-dwellers who occupied the area for thousands of years. Some show oversized human-like forms (some as tall as 2.7 metres/9 ft) with notable features such as triangular-shaped heads, missing or hollowed-out eyes and absent limbs. Other figures possess a ghostly quality or have strange bug-like eyes and antennae-like structures protruding from their heads.

Taken as a whole, the Barrier Canyon figures undeniably resemble modern depictions of space aliens – to a degree where some are convinced this is exactly what they show. Somewhere in the dim and distant past, they contend, ancient man played host to extraterrestrial visitors. The artwork preserves a record of that contact and may even have been created using techniques given to the indigenous population by their exotic guests.

The mainstream academic community, however, is more sanguine about what the artwork shows. One of the largest figures, designated the Barrier Canyon Holy Man, is surrounded by smaller figures, some of whom clutch snakes. These are not depictions of aliens, the naysayers claim, but of shamanistic visions that appeared to spiritual figureheads, probably during narcotic trances. The images are at once engrossing and disconcerting, and it may indeed be the product of what we might today call a 'bad trip'. Nonetheless, a small army of enthusiasts remain convinced that the rock art is proof that we are not alone in the Universe.

25 THE THIRD SECRET OF FÁTIMA

Between May and October 1917, three young Portuguese girls – Lúcia Santos, Jacinta Marto and Francisco Marto – reported visitations from the Virgin Mary, who revealed three secrets to them. The first two were made public in the 1940s, but the third was to be revealed only in 1960. In the event, it was not released until 2000, and there are many who claim that even then it was falsified or only partial.

The apparent visitations (six in total) occurred to the girls on a hillside not far from the town of Fátima. The first secret involved a vision of Hell widely interpreted as relating to the two World Wars. The second was thought to presage the Russian state's return to Christianity. The third secret, however, was apparently deemed too incendiary for contemporaneous release.

Lúcia, who wrote the secret down, is said to have believed that by 1960 it would be more readily understood. However, come that year, the Vatican issued a press release stating it was 'most probable the Secret would remain, forever, under absolute seal'. Such a declaration inevitably provoked speculation: what could be so sensitive that it might never be shared? In the Cold War age, thoughts immediately turned to prophecies of Armageddon, while some commentators wondered whether the Church itself faced some shocking revelation.

After four further decades of rumour and innuendo, Pope John Paul II agreed to publish the Third Secret in 2000. It left many distinctly underwhelmed: in an allegory dealing apparently with martyrdom and suffering, a man in white clothes falls to the ground dead. Had it, some wondered, foretold the attempted assassination of John Paul, on the anniversary of the first apparition in 1981? But even if that was the case, did it explain the Vatican's previous assertion that the secret might never be revealed? Many doubted it. So was this really the Third Secret, commentators wondered, and if so, was it the entire revelation? Other observers noted that the published secret took the form of a four-page text, while Lúcia supposedly wrote her account on a single sheet. Furthermore, wasn't it supposed to contain words directly from the Virgin Mary? In the Vatican edition, there were none.

The Vatican contends that the Third Secret was published in its entirety in 2000. Some will happily take their word on that, yet previous reluctance to share the confidence leads others to wonder if all is still not quite as it seems.

DISAPPEARANCES
AND VANISHINGS

26 THE LOST VILLAGE AT ANJIKUNI LAKE

Nunavut, part of Canada's Northwest Territories until 1999, is a vast territory covering the upper reaches of the country. Its population is small and sparsely distributed, its landscape desolate, icy and unwelcoming. If you get lost in this neck of the woods, don't anticipate stumbling upon a friendly face any time soon. But did the population of a local village *really* disappear without trace back in 1930?

G iven the uncompromising conditions they faced, it's little wonder that itinerant trappers made sure to know the location of rare permanent settlements where they might hole up for a night. One of these places, it is said, was Anjikuni, an Inuit fishing village on the Kazan River.

The story goes that Anjikuni was known to a trapper called Joe Labelle. But when he arrived here one evening in 1930, he stumbled upon a disturbing scene. All of the villagers (around 25 in total) had disappeared, as if into thin air. Food still hung over fire pits, clothing had been abandoned mid-repair, valuables and essentials lay untouched, and seven dogs had been abandoned to their fates. Labelle was said to have informed the Royal Canadian Mounted Police (RCMP) of his discovery, but they were unable to find any trace of the missing population.

The story was soon related by journalist Emmet E. Kelleher in *The Bee*, a newspaper in Danville, Virginia, but went strangely unreported in the Canadian press. Resurrected by Frank Edwards in his 1959 book, *Stranger than Fiction*, it took on a life of its own, and by the 1970s there was much speculation as to the villagers' fate. Among the more fanciful suggestions were vampire attack and alien abduction.

The RCMP issued a statement denying there had ever been such an incident, doubting that the village even existed, and denying they had ever investigated the claims. But this last seems to conflict with a report from January 1931, apparently released by the then-Commissioner of the RCMP, dismissing the episode as a journalistic hoax following investigations by one Sergeant J. Nelson. Others have suggested that the real cover-up was perpetrated by the authorities, who discovered some truth too terrible to relate.

Today, it is no easy job to tell who was pulling the wool over whose eyes back in 1930. Was the story of Anjikuni simply a feat of imagination by a hack in need of good copy, or was there something more sinister at work?

27 THE DISAPPEARANCE OF JUDGE CRATER

A dapper judge in New York's Supreme Court, Joseph Crater seemed to have it all – but still he wanted more. Having achieved so much so young, he was rumoured to be immersed in the grubbier aspects of City Hall politics. Despite being married, he was also known to have an eye for the ladies. Did his extracurricular activities upset someone who took their revenge by plucking him from the streets of the Big Apple?

Crater worked hard to establish his career after graduating from New York's Columbia University in 1916, and built up a network of powerful friends. In April 1930, he was appointed an Associate Justice of the New York Supreme Court by then-governor and future president, Franklin D. Roosevelt – a surprise appointment given that he was not the leading candidate. Those of a cynical bent went as far as to suggest Crater had paid off the city's political bosses (who operated out of the legendary Tammany Hall) to secure the job.

At the end of July, while on vacation with his wife Stella in Maine, Crater received a phone call one evening that left him visibly shaken. Refusing to tell Stella who had called and why, he said only that he needed to return to New York to 'straighten those fellows out'. Sure enough, the next day he travelled to his apartment on Fifth Avenue, but then headed for Atlantic City with his lover, a showgirl called Sally Lou Ritzi. He was back in New York by 3 August and spent most of 6 August in his office, sorting through personal files and allegedly destroying papers. He also cashed two cheques that together were worth over US$5,000 (more than US$75,000 in today's money) and made for home with two locked suitcases.

That evening, Crater went for dinner at Billy Haas's Chophouse with Ritzi and William Klein, a lawyer friend. They left him at 9.30 p.m., when Crater apparently headed off to the theatre. It was the last that was ever seen of the judge, although he was not missed for a week and a half. His friends and colleagues believed he was on holiday, while Stella apparently assumed he was taken up with business.

It was only on 3 September that police were brought in to investigate. Once the story broke, it caused a sensation. There were sightings of Crater, now known as 'the missingest man in New York', up and down the country. None proved genuine and succeeded only in using up valuable police resources. Detectives did, however, discover that Crater's two mysterious suitcases were missing, and a safety deposit box belonging to him had been emptied too. Nonetheless, they failed to make the crucial breakthrough and in October 1930 a Grand Jury concluded: 'The evidence is insufficient to warrant any expression of opinion as to whether Crater is alive or dead, or as to whether he has absented himself voluntarily, or is the sufferer from disease in the nature of amnesia, or is the victim of crime.' Crater was legally declared dead in 1939 and the police finally closed the case file in 1979.

Theories abound as to the Judge's fate. There are some who believe he engineered a 'moonlight flit', perhaps to make a new life with one of his many lady friends (and a bundle of pilfered cash). Alternatively, perhaps he had got in over his head on some dodgy deal involving his friends from Tammany Hall. Although his involvement in government corruption was never proven, there is considerable circumstantial evidence that his hands were far from clean. Might he have committed suicide, fearing the net was closing in?

His widow, among others, was convinced he was murdered, with Stella believing that a good-time girl with underworld connections had been trying to blackmail him. For a while suspicion fell upon the notorious gangster Jack 'Legs' Diamond, a known associate of Crater. Had their relationship turned sour? There was briefly talk that Diamond had dispatched Crater in an upstate brewery, but the charges never stuck.

Then in 2005, a 91-year-old woman, Stella Ferrucci-Good, died in Queens, leaving behind a note not to be opened in her lifetime. In it she claimed that her long-deceased husband, Robert Good, plus a New York cop called Charles Burns, along with his brother Frank, a cabbie, had killed Crater and dumped the body on Coney Island. While their motive was not clear, there was a suggestion that Officer Burns at least had mob connections. Although the police took the second-hand confession seriously, they have thus far been unable to confirm its veracity.

Crater undoubtedly inhabited a shady world, counting gangsters, ladies of the night and the Tammany Hall crew among its cast. Whether he was put out of the way deliberately, or decided to take his leave of his own accord, it's likely that many of his associates were glad to see the back of him.

28 JIMMY HOFFA

On 30 July 1975, arguably the most powerful union leader that the United States had ever seen went missing from the car park of the Machus Red Fox Restaurant in a well-to-do suburb of Detroit. It is believed that he was scheduled to meet with two prominent gangsters, but Hoffa was never seen again. The murky details of his life, and speculation as to the nature of its end, have fascinated ever since.

Born on 14 February 1913 in the town of Brazil, Indiana, Jimmy Hoffa left school when he was aged 14. He began working for a local grocer, barely scraping a living wage and labouring under unacceptable conditions. Refusing to accept his lot, he set about organizing his fellow workers in a bid to assert their rights. His colleagues, many of them much older than Hoffa, were soon impressed by his passionate campaigning. By the time he was in his mid-20s, Hoffa had become one of the leading figures in the International Brotherhood of Teamsters (IBT), a union representing truck drivers and warehouse labourers. In 1958, after six years as IBT vice president, he became its president, serving in the post for 13 years and overseeing a membership boom that left him responsible for 1,500,000 workers.

To many he was a hero, fighting hard to improve the working lives of his union members and standing up for the civil rights movement. However, there was also a dark side to his career. From the outset, much of the trucking business in the US was under the control of organized crime. In order to ensure his own position and to fight on behalf of his IBT members, Hoffa metaphorically got into bed with some very unpleasant characters.

Unsurprisingly, he also made powerful enemies who yearned to bring him down. When John F. Kennedy entered the White House in 1960, he appointed his brother Bobby as attorney general, with a remit to take on organized crime. Sure enough, having dodged several legal bullets, in 1964, Hoffa was finally convicted on criminal charges relating to the attempted bribery of a grand juror. He received a prison sentence of eight years.

A few months later came another conviction, this time for misuse of the union pension fund (which had been raided to provide loans to underworld figures). A five-year sentence was added to the eight-year stretch he was already serving. However, in late 1971 President Richard Nixon reached an agreement that saw Hoffa freed from jail on condition that he stayed out of union activism until 1980.

But it was not only the White House that wanted to curb Hoffa's activities – there were many within the union movement itself who felt that he had had his day. Nonetheless, he remained a significant public figure until, one July lunchtime in 1975, he was last seen at the Machus Red Fox Restaurant. It is alleged that he had told associates he was to meet two reported mobsters there, Antony Giacalone and Antony Provenzano. Both, however, denied that any such meeting either took place or was scheduled. Hoffa's car, a 1974 Pontiac Grand Ville, was discovered unlocked in the restaurant car park but there were no clues as to the nature of Hoffa's fate.

The rumour mill went into overdrive. Was this the settling of an old score? Did organized criminals see Hoffa's desire to make a political comeback as a threat to their own unionized revenue streams? Some have even suggested that Hoffa faked his own disappearance so that he could dance off into the sunset to enjoy his ill-gotten gains. Most, however, believe that Hoffa was almost certainly killed at the behest of one or other underworld figure, and so, seven years to the day after his disappearance, he was legally declared dead. There have been several attempts over the years to recover his body, usually following some tip-off or other, but so far the search has proved fruitless. It has been alleged that his half-burnt body was concealed in a large oil drum that was stored in the boot of a car subsequently compacted and sent to the Far East for scrap. Alternatively, in 2013 a source close to the ongoing investigation reported that Hoffa's body had been broken down into irrecoverable pieces in a wood chipper.

Jimmy Hoffa was an abrasive and hugely divisive figure who lived dangerously and rubbed shoulders with many ruthless people. He was a man, too, who was in possession of explosive secrets. Perhaps it is little surprise that he came to a nasty end. But knowing exactly who it was that did for him and why are questions whose answers remain as elusive now as they were on the day he went missing.

29 THE VALENTICH INCIDENT

Frederick Valentich, a 20-year-old would-be hotshot pilot, was on a training flight in 1978 when he radioed to Melbourne air traffic control to report an unidentified flying object speeding through the sky above him. Suddenly, all contact was lost, and no trace of Valentich was ever found. Was he the victim of an accident, did he have a hand in his own fate or were there third parties involved?

Valentich had some 150 hours of cockpit experience when he took off in his Cessna aircraft on 21 October 1978. Just after 7 p.m. he reported an unidentified aircraft about 300 metres (1,000 ft) above him, but the control tower found no traffic in that area. Valentich described a shiny metallic craft with a green light – he suspected its pilot was toying with him. Furthermore, the Cessna was displaying engine trouble. When asked to identify the other aircraft, he replied 'It isn't an aircraft. It is . . .' Then his voice cut out. A couple of minutes later, contact was lost altogether. Air traffic control reported hearing a metallic clanging sound and then Valentich was gone.

Over four days, searchers scanned an area of 2,500 square kilometres (1,000 square miles) but found nothing. A Department of Transport investigation was unable to determine the cause of the disappearance but said it was 'presumed fatal'. UFOlogists seized on the incident – here, surely, was proof of an attack from a hostile UFO? There was even speculation about alien abduction.

But the fact that Valentich was himself a believer in UFOs raised alarm bells with others. Some observers pondered whether he had staged the episode – a thesis that became less likely after wreckage found in the Bass Strait in 1983 was identified as a possible match for his plane. Suggestions that he was intent on suicide and determined to go out in style met with scepticism from friends and family. Another theory was that he had simply become disorientated, perhaps inadvertently turning his plane upside-down or going into a so-called 'graveyard spiral', so that the 'UFO' was merely his Cessna's reflection in the water below or his misinterpretation of natural light from celestial bodies.

The Department of Transport's original report only came to light years after investigators had been told it was lost – was there a deliberate attempt to bury it? Intriguingly, it includes a suggestion that the Ministry of Defence should launch an inquiry into possible UFO involvement. Should Valentich be taken at his word after all?

30 JEAN SPANGLER

Spangler was the classic movie wannabe – in her mid-20s, blue-eyed and sultry; a few bit-part film appearances had brought her close to the stars, but stardom in her own right remained elusive. Divorced and with a young child, she left home one evening in autumn 1949, apparently to rendezvous with her ex-husband. She was never seen again, though her purse was found shortly afterwards containing a cryptic message.

Jean Elizabeth Spangler was born in Seattle, Washington, on 2 September 1923 and made her way in the world as a part-time model and dancer at various nightspots. In 1942, she began a turbulent and unhappy marriage to one Dexter Benner, whom she petitioned for divorce on the grounds of cruelty after only six months. Despite this, they stayed together for some four years, during which time she gave birth to his daughter, Christine.

A fierce custody battle played out after the couple finally divorced in 1946, with Spangler eventually emerging victorious and taking her daughter to live in an apartment with her mother, brother and sister-in-law in the Park La Brea neighbourhood close to Los Angeles' Wilshire Boulevard. Within a couple of years, Jean would take an uncredited role in the movie *Miracle of the Bells*, the first of seven films in which she appeared.

On 7 October 1949, at around five in the evening, Jean left home, telling her brother's wife, Sophie, that she was going to meet Benner to discuss the late arrival of a child-support payment. From there, she said, she would continue to the night-shoot for a film she was working on. The last known sighting of Jean Spangler came just an hour later, when a clerk at a local store noticed her apparently waiting for someone. When she failed to return home the following day, Sophie filed a missing-person's case with the local police.

Needless to say, Dexter Benner was immediately treated as a prime suspect, but he told the police that he had not seen his wife for several weeks – an alibi that was corroborated by his new spouse. Further investigations also revealed that there was no movie shooting on that night that had expected Jean on its set. Her family, meanwhile, were adamant that she wouldn't simply have left town of her own accord because she cared too much for her child.

A clue emerged the following day, 9 October, when Jean's purse was discovered close to one of the entrances of LA's Griffith Park. Its straps were torn, suggesting that it might have been wrenched from its owner's grasp, but the penurious Jean was known to have had no money in the purse, so robbery seemed an unlikely scenario. The purse did, however, contain one item of interest: a note that read 'Kirk, Can't wait any longer. Going to see Dr Scott. It will work best this way while mother is away.' (Jean's mother was indeed visiting Kentucky at the time of the disappearance). So who were Kirk and Dr Scott, and were either or both of them involved in whatever fate had befallen Jean?

By now, the press had sunk their teeth into the story, with the mysterious message appearing on newsstands up and down the land. It certainly caught the attention of one rather well-known individual – actor Kirk Douglas, who was shortly to be Oscar-nominated for his role in 1949's

Champion. Douglas realized that Jean had been an extra in one of his recent movies (the implausibly titled *Young Man with a Horn*). He promptly contacted the police to assure them that he knew her only in passing and was certainly not the Kirk referred to in the letter. Of course, he had propelled himself on to the police radar but they were, as he had hoped, quick to clear him.

Attempts to trace the actual Kirk or the mysterious Dr Scott proved unsuccessful. Spangler had previously dated a 'Scotty' who worked in the Army Air Corps (and who had beaten and threatened her when she ended their relationship four years earlier), but the link was tenuous at best. There was also a shady figure known as 'Doc' that the police heard about in some of the Sunset Strip bars where Jean used to socialize. It was alleged that he carried out illegal abortions for a price, and there were rumours that Jean was indeed in the early stages of pregnancy when she disappeared.

There was even talk that she had got in a little too deep with a couple of henchmen of a notorious gangster, Mickey Cohen. Both the henchmen vanished – presumed murdered – within a few days of Jean's disappearance, leading some to suppose there was a connection, though it has never been proven. Subsequently, there were even reported sightings of Jean in the company of one of these hoodlums, Little Davy Ogul, in locations as disparate as California, Arizona and New Mexico. However, none was ever confirmed.

So the file on Jean Spangler remains open. With its cast of Hollywood hopefuls, fully fledged A-list stars, mobsters, angry exes and backstreet abortionists, her case has long held the public imagination. Alas, those able to furnish answers as to her fate are probably long dead themselves.

31 AMBROSE BIERCE

Ambrose Bierce was a military man, adventurer and writer. In late 1913, when he was in his early 70s, he took himself off to civil-war-torn Mexico. The last letter he ever sent is said to have concluded with the line: 'As to me, I leave here tomorrow for an unknown destination . . .' He was never seen again, and his curious disappearance provides American literature with one of its most enduring mysteries.

A mbrose Bierce was born in Ohio in 1842. When the Civil War arrived, he enlisted with the Union Army and saw front-line action – he was even mentioned in the newspapers for his role in rescuing a fellow soldier at the 1861 Battle of Rich Mountain while under fire.

In his later career as an author, meanwhile, he specialized in biting satirical journalism as well as short stories. His fiction was dark, and often tinged with horror – perhaps his most famous works were the astringent *The Devil's Dictionary* and the Civil War-set *An Occurrence at Owl Creek Bridge*. His personal life, meanwhile, was repeatedly touched by tragedy. Two of his three children failed to outlive him, his first son committing suicide in his late teens and his second son dying of pneumonia. His wife, meanwhile, died in 1905 just a few months after the couple had divorced.

In October 1913, the increasingly embittered (and heavy-drinking) Bierce began a tour of some of the areas he had seen during the Civil War, taking in Louisiana and Texas. He next went over the border into Mexico, which was then in its third year of brutal civil war. Tracing his movements beyond this becomes quite a challenge. On Boxing Day 1913, he is reputed to have written a letter to one of his dearest friends, Blanche Partington. It was this missive that supposedly contained the line about the 'unknown destination'.

Unfortunately, while there is significant circumstantial evidence that he did indeed write this letter, it has sadly not survived, leading some to speculate over the authenticity of that particular part of the tale. But whether Bierce wrote the letter or not, he was never heard of again. So what might have happened to him in Mexico?

One story has it that Bierce joined up as an observer with the army of prominent revolutionary general, Pancho Villa. He is said to have travelled with Villa's troops to Chihuahua, from where he sent the disputed letter to Blanche Partington. Some say he was then caught up in the rising tide of civil war violence, dying after putting himself in the way of danger once too often (possibly during a siege in early 1914). According to at least one source, federal troops killed him some time in 1914 when they learned of his association with Villa.

Others say that Villa himself had Bierce executed, after his sometime confidante became rather too outspoken in his criticisms. This was a line taken by one Adolph Danziger de Castro, author of an obscure 1928 biography of Bierce in which he claimed to have later met Villa and discussed the matter. Villa, according to de Castro, told him that Bierce would indulge in drunken, tequila-fuelled rants, with Villa treating 'his vapours with contempt'. 'I knew him,' Villa said ominously. 'He has passed.' Unfortunately, little is known of de Castro, and establishing the veracity of his account is all but impossible.

A few dissenting voices doubt that Bierce ever made it across the Rio Grande, suggesting that the trip to Mexico was an elaborate hoax. Instead, the speculation goes, he checked himself into an asylum in California and saw out his days living close to his beloved secretary. There are other, even more outlandish theories, including that he was a spy investigating international plots against the Panama Canal or that he had joined up with the famous British adventurer, F.A. Mitchell-Hedges (see page 201). The two, so the tale goes, worked their way through Mexico, accumulating Maya treasures as they went. Some versions of the story even have Bierce being held hostage by a local tribe so that they may worship him as a god.

An official inquiry instigated by the US government under pressure from Bierce's surviving daughter yielded nothing of note. Some have suggested that Bierce, facing old age and scarred by the many misfortunes that had befallen him over the years, decided to take his own life – certainly, he had made clear during his lifetime that he considered suicide a noble act. It has also been wryly noted on a good many occasions before now that suicide is not always a bad career option. In Bierce's case, death brought renewed attention to his work, and ensured a legacy of which he would doubtless have been proud. Fair reward, he might well have thought, for constructing an enigmatic mystery around his death.

32 BUSTER CRABB – MISSING IN ACTION

Lionel 'Buster' Crabb was a crack naval diver who earned his spurs during the Second World War and went on to carry out missions for the British secret services. In 1956, he was charged with leading a covert dive to investigate a Soviet ship docked at Portsmouth. He never emerged from the water, prompting decades of speculation as to what happened to him.

Born in 1909, Crabb joined the Royal Navy during the Second World War and trained as a diver. He worked first in Gibraltar in mine and bomb disposal, and then in Italy. He subsequently received the OBE and the George Cross in recognition of his brave service. He left the Navy for the first time in 1947 to become a civilian diver, but was back in the armed forces by the early 1950s before finally retiring in 1955. Not long after that, he was signed up by MI6, the foreign intelligence branch of the British secret services.

In April 1956, the Soviet leader Nikita Krushchev and his premier, Nikolai Bulganin, came to Britain on a diplomatic mission. They arrived on the cruiser *Ordzhonikidze*, which docked on the south coast of England at Portsmouth, a major naval dockyard. The British naval authorities were keen to learn more about the ship's radical new propeller design, and Crabb was assigned to secretly examine the vessel while it was conveniently located.

He stayed at the Sally Port Hotel in Portsmouth from 17 April, with a companion who signed the hotel register under the assumed name of Matthew Smith. On 19 April, Crabb sailed out into the harbour and made his dive. He never reappeared and ten days later the Admiralty reported him as missing, presumed dead. They claimed he had been engaged in testing new underwater equipment miles away from the Soviet ship when disaster struck. It was a piece of misdirection designed to avoid a diplomatic incident at a time when Downing Street was hoping to foster happier relations with the Soviets in the post-Stalin era.

But what had really happened? Was there a terrible accident or was Crabb killed deliberately? Alternatively, was he kidnapped by the Soviets, or might he have defected? Crabb, a smoker and drinker, was not at his physical peak in 1956. Given the intense physical exertion demanded by the mission, perhaps his body simply gave out or his equipment failed. Just over a year later, a body in diving gear washed up along the coast near Chichester in Sussex. Missing its head and hands (not uncommon for bodies in the water for prolonged periods), the corpse could not be positively identified by Crabb's ex-wife or his last girlfriend. Nonetheless, the body shared a number of physical similarities and was equipped with a diving suit like the one Crabb wore. The coroner was satisfied that Crabb had been found, but others had their doubts.

Official papers declassified in 2007 showed that Crabb had not dived alone that day. If the 'accidental death' theory is to be believed, we must accept that his unknown colleague or colleagues either did not spot him getting into difficulties, or were unable to assist him or raise an alarm in time.

Some have even speculated that he died at the hands of a diving companion. One theory goes that word had got out Crabb was planning to defect to the Russians, and fearing the embarrassment such an incident would cause the government, MI5 took it upon themselves to intervene decisively. Those who knew Crabb, however, doubt that such a patriot would ever 'turn to the dark side' – though stranger things have certainly happened.

Alternatively, was he killed by the Russians instead? Years later, a Soviet diver claimed to have found Crabb trying to plant a mine on the Ordzhonikidze and had cut his throat. However, his version of events is regarded with a certain scepticism given that the British authorities would surely not have imperilled a diplomatic mission in such a clumsy way. Others instead suggest that the crew of the *Ordzhonikidze* got wind of the spying mission and took Crabb prisoner, subsequently taking him to Moscow or, alternatively, setting him to work on their own secret underwater operations. There were even whispers that perhaps the whole episode was set up by MI6 in order for Crabb to be 'captured', so he could then serve as a double-agent.

Whether or not the British secret services knew exactly what had befallen their man, they certainly engineered a cover-up in order that details of his mission would remain hidden. Indeed, the episode caused a major rift between the UK's spymasters and Downing Street, with Prime Minister Anthony Eden only just falling short of describing his security services as out of control.

33 THE PRINCES IN THE TOWER

In April 1483, when Edward IV, King of England died, his son and heir, Edward, was only twelve years old, and his second son, Richard, Duke of York, nine. The dead king's brother, Richard, Duke of Gloucester, thus stepped in to fill the power vacuum. His nephews were kept at the Tower of London but by the end of the summer they had disappeared. The exact details of their fate remain hotly disputed.

Gloucester soon strengthened his own claim to the throne by having the young princes declared illegitimate. This was on the basis that his brother's marriage to their mother, Elizabeth Woodville, was illegal because Edward IV was pre-contracted to marry someone else. Gloucester was thus crowned as Richard III in July 1483. Over the next few months, Edward's sons were occasionally seen playing in the Tower grounds, but by the end of the summer all sightings ceased.

It was not long before rumours started that they had been slaughtered. Richard was the widely assumed culprit, since anyone intent on deposing him could choose no more suitable figureheads for a rebellion. Thomas More (Henry VIII's Chancellor) was among those convinced of Richard's guilt, claiming some 30 years after the fact that he had commissioned his loyal supporter Sir James Tyrrell to oversee the deed. According to More, Tyrrell hired two assassins, who smothered the boys in their beds.

Richard thus had opportunity and motive. Yet there are plenty of historians who doubt the theory's veracity. Why, for instance, would Elizabeth Woodville eventually make her peace with Richard if she truly believed (as she apparently once did) that he had murdered her beloved sons? It is possible she was being the ultimate pragmatist, reasoning that the best way to secure the futures of her remaining children was by bringing Richard onside – but could she really be that sanguine?

Then we must consider the lack of any concrete evidence that the boys were murdered. No bodies were ever produced by Richard's accusers, and certainly no 'smoking guns'. Richard's life was undoubtedly easier for their absence, but killing a king's sons is a risky business at the best of times. He may have justly reached the conclusion that he was best served by keeping the boys alive but out of sight. It has thus been suggested that he had them sent into exile in France, for instance, to be brought up with false identities.

A competing theory is that Edward did indeed die, but as the result of illness. We know that he was visited regularly by a doctor in the Tower – did he succumb to natural causes while his younger sibling survived? Did influential players know that the new king was no child-killer after all? This might explain why Woodville, for one, felt able to come to an understanding with Richard III. It would also account for why Richard was unable to simply produce the princes to counter claims that he was a murderer. (Aside from the fact that it served Richard well for people to suspect that his rival claimants to the throne were no more.)

And even if we accept that the boys were killed, Richard is far from the only person with motive. Henry VII, Richard's great rival and eventual successor as king, knew that the princes posed as much a threat to his claim on the throne as they did to their uncle's. The situation was further complicated when Henry married their eldest sister, Elizabeth of York, to strengthen his claim. In order for that to work, he had little choice but to revoke the law establishing the princes' illegitimacy, thus instantly increasing the threat they posed if still alive. In the cut-throat politics of the times, people were killed for far less. Henry also later seized the lands of his mother-in-law Elizabeth Woodville – was there a major falling-out between the two because Elizabeth learned of what he had done?

Alternative suspects include Henry's mother, Margaret Beaufort. Evidence against her is purely circumstantial, but she was infamously ruthless in pursuit of her son's interests. Others, meanwhile, have pointed the finger at the Duke of Buckingham. Once a close ally of Richard III, he was executed by the king in November 1483. Buckingham had been responsible for keeping the princes in custody, but had he taken his remit too far, leading to a devastating feud with his old friend? (Or, as has also been suggested, did their enmity originate from Buckingham's shock at learning that Richard had killed them?)

The role of Richard III in the fates of the little princes undoubtedly deserves to come under heavy scrutiny. However, his guilt for their murders cannot be assumed for two reasons – firstly, they might not have been murdered at all and, secondly, there are other strong suspects. Cool historical analysis reveals a large cast of ruthless political operators, all with good reason to cover up the truth.

34 THE MV *JOYITA*

On 10 November 1955, the merchant vessel *Joyita* was found abandoned in the South Pacific. It had been missing for several weeks but, while badly damaged and partially submerged, was still comfortably afloat. However, some four tonnes of its cargo were missing from its hold, as well as all hands. No trace of its passengers or crew was ever found – what drove them to abandon ship before rescue could arrive?

M V *Joyita* was originally built in 1931 as a 21.3-metre (70-ft) luxury yacht. Commissioned by a movie director who named it for his wife ('joyita' translating from Spanish as 'little jewel'), she was requisitioned by the US Navy in the Second World War, when it was based at Pearl Harbor and served as a patrol boat in the waters around Hawaii.

After the war, *Joyita* returned to civilian life, and by the 1950s she was being used as a fishing charter and for carrying light cargoes. She embarked on her ill-fated mission early in the morning of 3 October 1955, under the command of Captain 'Dusty' Miller. Sailing out of Samoa's capital city, Apia, she was headed for the Tokelau Islands, a little less than 480 kilometres (300 miles) away. The *Joyita* had a crew of sixteen plus nine passengers, including two children. She was carrying a mixture of medical supplies, food, timber and empty oil drums. It was expected that she would arrive at her destination within a couple of days, where she would be loaded with copra for the return journey.

After three days, therefore, the *Joyita* was reported late, although no distress call had been received. For six days a search-and-rescue party scoured some 260,000 square kilometres (100,000 square miles) of ocean, but to no avail. Almost a month after the search was called off, a merchant vessel discovered the *Joyita* drifting unmanned 1,000 kilometres (600 miles) from her intended route. She was listing heavily to the port side, and had suffered damage from taking on water, but her hull was intact. Lined extensively with cork and buoyed by the stock of empty drums, there was little prospect that she would sink.

However, alongside the passengers and crew, the boat's four dinghies and life-rafts were missing, as were the ship's log, much of its navigational equipment and some firearms that Captain Miller was known to keep with him. The on-board clocks were stopped at 10.25 and the lights were on, suggesting that whatever had transpired happened at night. A subsequent inquiry could not explain why everyone on board had trusted their survival to insubstantial rafts when the *Joyita* herself was almost certainly the safer bet. Their exodus was, in the words of an official report, 'inexplicable on the evidence submitted at the inquiry'.

Inevitably, there was frenzied speculation as to what had occurred. The boat had suffered some flooding – a result of fractured piping and failing bilge pumps – but Miller was experienced enough to know that there was no need to abandon ship. So what if he had not been in a state to communicate that message to the others on board? Some blood-stained bandages were recovered from the vessel, prompting suspicions that the captain had come to harm.

Had there been a mutiny? Miller's finances were under some stress, so perhaps he had insisted in continuing the trip when the crew thought it better to turn back or at least put in for repairs. It was well known that Miller did not get on at all well with his First Mate, Chuck Simpson – had they come to blows and gone overboard, or else caused serious injury to one another? If the boat then began to take on water at night, was there no one else to calm the situation until help arrived?

There were also suggestions of darker forces at play, and some of the wilder explanations may be put down to lingering post-war prejudice. The finger was pointed at unspecified Japanese fishermen, allegedly discovered by the *Joyita* while engaged in some nefarious activity. The normally reserved *Daily Telegraph* even suggested that renegade Japanese forces were responsible, convinced the war had not ended. Amid the fervour of the Cold War, others suggested that a Soviet submarine had kidnapped the vessel's inhabitants. But perhaps more likely is the suggestion that pirates were at work: it would certainly explain the absence of the cargo and the complete disappearance of all on board.

The boat was subsequently salvaged but ran aground twice before the decade was out. Perhaps taking the hint, *Joyita*'s owners beached her, and so ended the story of the sad little vessel. It seems certain that somebody did something they shouldn't have in 1955 and over two dozen people paid with their lives. But exactly who was the malefactor, and what was the nature of their crime, is as unclear today as it was back then.

35 THE MISSING NAZI GOLD

Brutal and wretched, the Second World War was also financially costly. To feed their war machine, the Nazis accumulated vast gold reserves, but with defeat imminent in 1945, they hid much of it away. Some disappeared with high-ranking individuals intent on new lives abroad, but a large amount was hidden by official order. In the years since 1945, countless treasure-seekers have gone in search of this lost wealth.

Throughout the late 1930s, rearmament had left Germany's limited gold reserves heavily depleted, but the outbreak of war in 1939 afforded the Nazi regime an opportunity to bolster them through assorted nefarious means. The treasuries of vanquished nations were plundered for all they were worth and, still worse, the extermination camps proved an invaluable source of wealth, as unfortunate victims were stripped of everything from wedding rings and watches to gold teeth.

While it is impossible to put an exact value on the Nazi's gold holdings, they would certainly have been measurable in terms of hundreds of tonnes. Some of this was used to pay for munitions and other supplies directly, but far more was laundered through Europe's banking system in return for foreign currency, with Switzerland the acknowledged hub for much of this activity. It is, for instance, estimated that some 100 tonnes of bullion was transferred to Swiss banks, with only four tonnes returned at the war's end.

Over the years, there have been many attempts through the courts to force these institutions to hand back what is, after all, stolen property, but such legal actions have met with limited success. The extent to which ostensibly respectable banks were involved in this murky world of laundering was brought into sharp focus in the 1990s, when a 1946 report by US Treasury agent Emerson Bigelow was declassified. Bigelow had concluded that no less an institution than the Vatican Bank had transferred large sums of confiscated Nazi gold into its accounts for 'safekeeping' – an allegation the Bank itself continues to refute.

It is clear that the chances of unpicking banking paper trails to track looted Nazi gold are slim in the extreme. For your average bounty hunter, the great hope lies in the prospect that the Nazis deposited significant amounts of gold not in bank accounts, but in physical hiding places in out-of-the-way locations. We know, for instance, that large volumes were hidden in defunct mines, such as the Merkers salt mine where US troops found a cache of gold as they advanced through Germany in 1945. There are strong rumours of such a hoard in the Leinawald Forest near Leipzig, but government attempts to recover the loot in the early 1960s failed, due to toxic gases emanating from nearby mines.

There is also a widely held belief that senior German officials ordered stolen loot be hidden in several lakes throughout Germany and Austria. While the precise details often died along with the men who gave the orders, it is suspected that Hermann Goering arranged for a stash to be emptied into Lake Stolpsee, north of Berlin. Pitifully, the task is said to have been carried out by concentration camp prisoners who, after deposited items including some 18 crates of gold and platinum, were then lined up on the lake's shore and shot

– a grotesque act presumably carried out at least in part to ensure the trove remained secret.

There is also significant circumstantial evidence that Lake Toplitz in Austria's Salzkammergut region was used as a dumping ground for gold worth billions in today's market. Contemporary witnesses claimed to have seen SS soldiers throwing metal crates into its icy waters in the last months of the war. Countless expeditions have attempted to recover this bounty, but Toplitz is some 90 metres (300 ft) deep and full of submerged logs, making diving perilous. Indeed, several people have been killed in the quest for its treasures. In 1959, a research team sent by *Stern* magazine failed to recover gold but did retrieve several crates of secret documents and counterfeit money along with a printing press. Today, treasure-hunters are strictly forbidden from entering the waters, though several continue to be apprehended each year.

While there have been sporadic discoveries of hidden Nazi troves – and there will presumably be more as time passes – it is striking just how effective the Nazi authorities were in hiding their ill-gotten gains. While plenty of prospectors are desperate to recover it, there are doubtless those who hope the booty remains lost forever, along with the horror stories attached to it.

36 GLENN MILLER

Forty-year-old Glenn Miller was the leader of the most popular Big Band of the age when he went missing in 1944. With hits to his name like 'In the Mood', he spent much of the Second World War performing in front of troops to bolster morale. His complete disappearance while flying to play for allied forces in France gave rise to a glut of conspiracy theories about his fate.

On 15 December, a particularly cold and foggy day, Miller was flying in a Noorduyn 'Norseman' C-64 aeroplane from England to Paris. According to the official story, the plane got into trouble somewhere over the Channel, probably as a result of engine failure or else ice on the wings. It is then thought to have ditched into the sea, killing all on board.

Yet, neither the wreckage of the aircraft nor the bodies of its occupants was ever recovered. Miller's own brother, Herb, suggested in the 1980s that Glenn had been suffering from lung cancer and had died in a military hospital a few days after landing in France. He contended that the crash story was invented to fulfil Glenn's wish to 'die as a hero and not in a lousy bed'. But despite its provenance, there is little hard evidence to back the claim. An alternative hypothesis is that he was involved in espionage (some sources even suggesting he was working in tandem with the great British actor, David Niven). But suggestions that Miller was killed working as a spy are seen as highly dubious by most commentators.

There is also a widely discredited theory that Miller made it safely to France but then died in a compromising situation while associating with a Parisian prostitute. In a bid to avoid a dangerous knock to wartime morale, the thesis continues, the Allied powers set about orchestrating an elaborate cover-up. A more credible suggestion is that the Norseman was downed by friendly fire. There is certainly evidence that a squadron of British Lancaster bombers ditched their payload over the Channel that day after an aborted bombing raid over Germany. There were even eye-witness reports of a plane disappearing into the water. However, several analysts have argued it is unlikely that the Norseman would have been in the relevant locale at the right time.

Of course, there are also many who believe that Miller was simply the victim of a tragedy, just as the official investigation suggested. But in the absence of a wreck or a body, the question of what happened to the King of Swing will continue to be asked.

37 LOUIS LE PRINCE

Louis Le Prince is one of the forgotten names from the early days of motion pictures, but to some he is nothing less than the 'Father of Cinematography'. In 1890, he went missing in his native France, shortly before he was scheduled to travel to the United States to demonstrate his great invention. What befell him remains a mystery, but the stench of foul play hangs heavy over the tale.

In 1886, Le Prince took a job in Leeds, England, where he married before moving to New York. There he pondered how he might create moving pictures. By 1888, he had invented a workable single-lens camera, which he used to capture footage around Leeds. Arguably, this was the birth of cinema: he promptly made arrangements to project the film in New York late in 1890 – four years before Thomas Edison opened his first kinematograph parlour.

In September 1890, Le Prince was in France, and due to take a train from Dijon to Paris. His brother reported seeing him off at Dijon Station, but when the train arrived at its destination there was no sign of either Le Prince or his luggage. Had he, as some suggested, committed the 'perfect' suicide owing to disastrous finances? It seems unlikely, given that his cinematic breakthrough promised him a fortune. An alternative theory was that he had assumed a new life in Chicago after his family learned he was gay, although corroborating evidence is scant. Or might his brother, the last person to see him alive, have done for his sibling for personal or financial reasons that remain unclear? But perhaps the most intriguing premise is that Le Prince was assassinated to prevent him from patenting his cinematographic equipment.

It is known that he was bound for the UK to register a patent, with his New York trip booked for shortly after. It is also true that his family later became embroiled in a long-running legal dispute with Edison over the invention of cinematography. Having disappeared, Le Prince was not considered legally dead by the US justice system for seven years, holding up the family's civil actions. However, after the courts found for Edison in 1901, the verdict was overturned the following year: Edison was not the sole inventor. By then Le Prince's son, Adolphus – a key witness in the dispute – was also dead from gunshot wounds. His mother was convinced this was the second murder the family had suffered, all for the sake of their interest in the movies.

38 AGATHA CHRISTIE – THE LADY VANISHES

Agatha Christie was at her best exploring the darker side of human nature. In some 80 crime novels and short-story collections starring the likes of Miss Marple, Hercule Poirot and Tommy & Tuppence, she became a household name, with accumulated book sales estimated to be in excess of two billion. Unsurprisingly then, her brief and unexplained disappearance in late 1926 caused a sensation.

C hristie, who had shot to fame six years earlier with the publication of *The Mysterious Affair at Styles,* was in the twelfth year of an unhappy marriage to Colonel Archibald Christie. After a heated row at their Berkshire home on 3 December 1926, he left to spend the weekend with his long-term lover, Nancy Neele. Agatha, meanwhile, informed her secretary that she was going to Yorkshire, leaving that same evening. But it was not long before her car, a Morris Cowley, was found at Newlands Corner in Surrey. Inside was an expired driving licence and some clothes. Of the lady herself, there was no sign. It was just like a plot from one of her bestsellers – and the nation was suitably gripped.

The immediate speculation was that she had decided to end it all, drowning herself at a nearby spring called Silent Pool. Then came the suggestion of foul play, with her husband as prime suspect. A thousand police officers and thousands more volunteers searched in vain, and it took an eagle-eyed banjo player by the name of Bob Tappin to find her, holed up at the Swan Hydropathic Hotel in Harrogate, Yorkshire. She had booked herself in under a pseudonym, Mrs Teresa Neele of Cape Town – it was surely no coincidence that she had adopted the surname of her love rival.

With Colonel Christie in the clear, the public thirsted for an explanation. Agatha was diagnosed with amnesia. She was undoubtedly under severe strain at the time: not only was her marriage falling apart, she was also chronically overworked and had recently lost her mother.

But not everyone was satisfied that she was simply not in control of her mental faculties. Some suspected an outrageous publicity stunt. Others accused her of trying to frame her spouse. Christie herself never provided an explanation, failing to mention the episode entirely in her later autobiography. Whether it was a chronic amnesiac episode or something more calculated, she certainly wasn't sharing. And who could expect anything else from the true Queen of Mystery?

39 JIM THOMPSON

The professional life of Jim Thompson had two very distinct phases. The first involved work in the US Office of Strategic Services, forerunner of the CIA. Then, after the Second World War, he established himself as saviour of Thailand's silk industry, making himself extremely rich in the process. In early 1967, he went for a walk in the Malaysian countryside and was never seen again. Had his old life caught up with him?

Thompson firmly believed in America's post-war mission to spread democracy around the world. Thus, he found himself in southeast Asia, often working without official authorization to support the region's burgeoning rebel groups. However, he came to believe that the US government was too intent on backing any enemies of communism, regardless of democratic credentials.

Having settled in Bangkok, Thompson took a dramatic new direction in 1948, setting up his Thai Silk Company. Employing modern techniques and paying fair wages, the firm boomed, earning him the nickname, 'the Silk King'. On 26 March 1967, he was staying with friends at a cottage in Malaysia's Cameron Highlands. At around 3 p.m. he went for a walk, but apparently planned a swift return, since he left behind his jacket, medication and cigarettes. When there was no sign of him by late evening, his companions reported him missing. Given his celebrity, the police promptly launched a search on an unprecedented scale, but failed to find him.

The official line was that he had probably become lost in the jungle or fallen down a ravine – he might even have been attacked by a tiger. But few who knew him believed the seasoned ex-spy couldn't navigate an afternoon stroll. Others suggested that he staged his disappearance to avoid being outed as gay or, alternatively, as a double agent. However, many students of the case are convinced Thompson never entirely broke his ties with US intelligence: they wonder whether he was brought in for 'one last mission' that went wrong. Or was he disposed of by those on his own side who considered he had become a liability? It is reported, for instance, that the FBI had previously investigated him for 'un-American activities'.

There were also rumours of a local man's deathbed confession: Thompson had died in a road accident and the local had quietly buried the body without reporting the incident. Maybe the King of Silk did meet such a banal ending, but the suspicion lingers that there was more to it than that.

40 ARTHUR CRAVAN

Variously a poet, artist, fighter, singer and 'citizen of twenty countries', Arthur Cravan treated his life as a piece of performance art, getting himself into countless scrapes and never being afraid to shock. Finding himself in Mexico at the end of the First World War, he planned to sail for Argentina to rendezvous with his wife, but he was never seen again, and not everyone is convinced that he died beneath the waves.

The name Arthur Cravan was itself a fiction – a pseudonym adopted by Fabian Avenarius Lloyd. After apparently being expelled from an English military school, Lloyd changed his name in 1912 (one of several identities he assumed during his lifetime). Over the next few years he travelled extensively in Europe and America, editing an influential cultural magazine, *Maintenant!*, and writing occasionally offensive poetry. He was also famed for putting on public performances that regularly descended into chaos. At one event in Paris in 1914 he promised to execute himself on stage with a revolver. Two years later he found himself in Spain fighting the world heavyweight boxing champion, Jack Johnson. The fight was over, predictably, in the blink of an eye, with Johnson speculating that his opponent was 'out of training'.

In 1914, Cravan travelled to the US, where he met his future wife, the poet Mina Loy. In 1917, he was present at the New York Society of Independent Artists exhibition where Marcel Duchamp launched the era of modern art with his signed urinal. At the same event, a drunk Cravan was wrestled off stage by police as he tried to strip naked while giving a lecture. When the US entered the war in 1917, he and Mina moved to Mexico. In November 1918, they planned to visit Argentina but could afford only one regular ticket. So Cravan determined to meet his wife there after sailing himself in a small sailboat. Alas, their reunion never took place. It was assumed he had capsized and drowned en route from Mexico but no body was recovered.

For decades afterwards, there were sporadic reports of sightings from around the world. Cravan had long been intrigued by the idea of faking his death, so there is a suspicion that they might be credible. There has even been work posthumously attributed to him, with speculation that he may have been the enigmatic writer B. Traven, whose novels include 1927's *The Treasure of the Sierra Madre*. Certainly, no man would have taken more delight than Cravan in deflecting the truth surrounding his fate.

MURDER MOST FOUL AND DEATHS UNACCOUNTABLE

41 THE BLACK DAHLIA MURDER

On 15 January 1947, Betty Bersinger and her young child went for a walk in Leimert Park in South Los Angeles. Betty spied what she thought was a shop mannequin in a vacant lot on Norton Avenue, just between 39th and Coliseum Streets. In fact, it was the naked and mutilated corpse of 22-year-old Elizabeth Short. So began a murder inquiry that continues to fascinate to this day.

Elizabeth Short's brief life was blighted by misfortune. Born in Boston on 29 July 1924, she had endured a troubled childhood beset with ill health and marked by a parental split – in fact, her father faked his suicide. It was little surprise, then, that she went off the rails a little, as evidenced by her early run-in with the law for underage drinking.

Thereafter, she drifted around the country from Massachusetts to Florida before ending up in southern California. She supported herself by waitressing, although work was far from regular. But as a petite, blue-eyed brunette, she had little trouble in attracting men and was not averse to hooking up with suitors willing to splash the cash. After her death, this gave rise to rumours that she had been a call girl of some sort, but there has never been any conclusive evidence to substantiate this claim.

In fact, there are counterclaims that she had suffered some medical complications that led to intimacy being something of a rarity for her. There is no doubt that she had a great many boyfriends, but several of these would subsequently report a similar tale: they would wine and dine Elizabeth before she would make her excuses and leave.

By early 1947, Elizabeth was severely short of cash, and struggling to pay even the meagre rent for the doss houses she'd been staying in. But Betty Bersinger's macabre discovery turned her into an overnight sensation – albeit a tragic one. Short's body had been cut in two at the waist, drained of blood and then portions of flesh had been removed. The cadaver had been washed and posed, the hands positioned over the head and the legs spread. A 'smile' had been carved into her face from the corners of her mouth up to her ears, and there were ligature marks on her arms, legs and neck.

An autopsy gave the cause of death as haemorrhaging from cuts to the face, allied to shock from blows to the head. The media had a field day and it was not long before Elizabeth had been renamed as the 'Black Dahlia'. Some claimed this was her nickname, perhaps making reference to a popular film noir of the time, *The Blue Dahlia*. Others suggested the name was entirely a journalistic creation, but whatever its origins, it stuck all the same.

On 23 January 1947, Short's supposed killer wrote to the *Los Angeles Examiner*, and there was soon an entire queue of cranks and attention-seekers prepared to take responsibility for the crime. Most of them, the Los Angeles Police Department were quickly able to dismiss. But then in early February, the same newspaper received a package containing a number of Elizabeth's personal effects, including an address book containing contact details for some 75 men. All were traced and interviewed, but no one was charged.

What the police really wanted to know was what had happened in the 'missing week' before her death. Robert 'Red' Manley reported leaving her in the lobby of the glamorous Biltmore Hotel on 9 January, and was long considered a prime suspect before he passed a polygraph test. Others who came under suspicion included Mark Hansen, a low-rent nightclub owner with whom Short had stayed for several months in 1946 and whose attentions she was said to have rejected. Then there was Jack Anderson Wilson, an alcoholic drifter who supposedly provided author John Gilmore with details of the crime that only the killer could have known, but who died in a hotel fire before he could be arrested and questioned.

In 1997, *LA Times* writer Larry Harnisch accused Dr Walter Alonzo Bayley, a surgeon who lived close to the crime scene and whose daughter was friends with Short's sister. Harnisch claimed Bayley suffered mental problems that drove him to kill, but Bayley was 67 at the time of the killing, with no record of such behaviour. Meanwhile, in 2003, Steve Hodel, previously an LAPD detective, pointed the finger at his father, Dr George Hodel. Certainly, the police became convinced that the killer must have been a medical man, given what had been done to the body. It has even been somewhat ludicrously suggested that Orson Welles was the real culprit.

With the passage of time and decaying evidence, this is a crime now unlikely to ever be solved, leaving the Black Dahlia as a pitiful symbol of a bygone era.

42 THE DYATLOV PASS INCIDENT

In 1959, nine cross-country skiers went missing in Russia's Ural Mountains. Over a period of ten weeks their bodies were recovered and all the evidence pointed to them having been running away from something terrifying. But just what was it? The finger of blame has been variously pointed at outer space, the Soviet military and Mother Nature.

The trip began in late January 1959 and was led by Igor Dyatlov (after whom the pass where the tragedy happened was later renamed). He had gathered ten doughty adventurers (eight men and two women) from the Ural Polytechnic Institute with the aim of skiing to Otorten Mountain in the northern Urals. They travelled by train to the city of Ivdel in Sverdlovsk Oblast and from there took a truck to Vizhai, the last point of civilization until Otorten. They started their long ski on 27 January, but within a day, one of the men was forced to turn back owing to ill health. By 1 February, the others had reached the eastern side of Kholat Syakhyl ('Dead Mountain'). Though they had strayed slightly off their planned course, the group decided to set up camp there for the night.

Dyatlov had arranged to make contact with friends back at the Institute once the expedition had safely returned to Vizhai. When there was no word by 20 February, a team of volunteers began a search and were soon joined by the police and army. Six days later, they found the abandoned camp at Kholat Syakhyl. The tent, which had been ripped open from the inside, was badly damaged and covered in snow. Wherever the adventurers had gone, they had left their belongings behind. Tracks in the snow indicated that Dyatlov and his crew had left in a hurry – some barefoot and others wearing only socks.

Shortly afterwards, five bodies were discovered within a few hundred metres of the camp in various states of undress. Some seemed to have been fleeing, while others might have been attempting to return. The remaining four bodies were not recovered until 4 May, hidden under deep snow in a ravine. They were generally better dressed than the first five, though some were wearing clothes that did not belong to them.

While it was ruled that the first five victims had all died from hypothermia, the case of the other four was more complicated. While none showed signs of external injuries, three of them had major damage to either the head or chest caused by an impact of the type one might expect in a car crash, Meanwhile, one of them, Lyudmila Dubinina, had lost her tongue. An official enquiry concluded that the nine had died as the result of 'a compelling natural force' – a judgment that left plenty of room for speculation.

Initially, some accused the local Mansi people of a wretched crime. However, few gave this theory much time. There was no sign of any other human presence in the area, and none of the bodies revealed evidence of soft-tissue damage. For similar reasons, animal attacks were also ruled out (though some have suggested a scavenger might have subsequently been responsible for taking Dubinina's tongue). At the time of the incident and for some weeks afterwards, there were reports from the region of orange spherical-like objects in the sky. This led to the suggestion that there may have been some extraterrestrial involvement in the deaths, or, alternatively, that the military were involved. Some have argued that these spheres were actually missiles and that the Soviets carried out extensive weapons testing in the area. This theory gained weight when some of the victims were found to have high levels of radioactive contamination. Furthermore, some attendees at the open-casket funerals of several victims reported the corpses as having discoloured skin.

Sceptics, though, point to the fact that such discolouration could simply have been the result of prolonged exposure to the elements and perhaps a heavy-handed mortician. Meanwhile, the radioactive contamination might be due to contact with thorium-based wicks commonly used in camping lanterns. The official files on the case only came into the public domain in the 1990s (and even then had a number of important omissions), so establishing the precise condition of the bodies and the extent of any contamination has been impossible.

Perhaps the most likely solution is that the group's camp was hit by a sudden avalanche. This would explain their rapid departure and unsuitable clothing. It would also account for why some showed signs only of hypothermia and exposure, while others suffered impact injuries. Yet this was not classic avalanche territory, and even if this thesis provides the best-fit answer, it leaves many questions unresolved.

43 THE SEVERED FEET OF THE NORTHWEST SEABOARD

The Salish Sea is a complex of waterways extending from southwest British Columbia in Canada to the northwest point of Washington State. On 20 August 2007, a girl spotted a size-12 trainer that had washed up on the shores of British Columbia's Jedediah Island. Inside was a sock, and inside that was a man's foot. It was the first in a series of macabre discoveries that gave rise to assorted dark theories.

I f that first find was disconcerting, the discovery of a second foot three weeks later – this time on Gabriola Island, also in British Columbia – provoked real concern. But this was just the start. Another foot was found on Valdes Island (BC) in February 2008, sparking a rush that saw a further four emerge by the end of the year (including, in August, the first on US shorelines).

As of May 2014, more than ten feet had been discovered on the coasts of British Columbia and a further four in Washington State. A grisly local mystery thus became the focus of international media attention, but there was little to go on – the feet originated from both males and females, were often in a state of decomposition, and were only linked by the fact that they were all discovered in sneaker-type footwear.

What initially seemed truly perplexing – why feet were turning up but no other body parts – was soon explained by science. The ankle being a relatively weak joint, it is not uncommon for feet to become detached from submerged cadavers. Encased in trainers that both served as both buoyancy aid and offered protection from hungry fish, the feet were duly able to travel across significant distances.

But whose feet were they? Early theories suggested they belonged to victims of some boating or air disaster, although the sheer number of recovered examples came to undermine the notion. When it was pointed out that most of the footwear pre-dated 2004, it was suggested that perhaps these were victims of the 2004 Asian tsunami. Others, meanwhile, saw only foul play at work – either a maniac lone murderer, a failed people-smuggling operation or perhaps the Mafia sending terrifying warning messages.

A few of the feet have been identified as belonging variously to suicidees and victims of accidents (one as long ago as 1987). But for observers who see something more sinister at play, the game is afoot.

44 THE STRANGE DEATH OF EDGAR ALLAN POE

As author of stories including *The Murders in the Rue Morgue* and *The Purloined Letter*, Edgar Allan Poe was an early master of the literary mystery. Yet perhaps the greatest mystery he bequeathed us is the one surrounding his death. In October 1840, he was discovered in Baltimore in a dishevelled state and never recovered. But how did he come to be in such a vulnerable condition?

O n 3 October 1840, one Joseph Walker came across Poe outside a tavern, apparently delirious and, in Walker's own words, 'in great distress' and 'in need of immediate assistance'. Walker contacted Dr Joseph Snodgrass, who knew the author, and Poe was soon under the care of Dr John Joseph Moran at Washington College Hospital. There he was kept in a private room without visitors, unable to provide a coherent explanation of what had happened to him. At 5 a.m. on 7 October, he passed away, aged just 40.

Most of our knowledge of Poe's final days comes from recollections of Snodgrass and Moran. Snodgrass described his 'repulsive' appearance – his hair was a great, unkempt mess, his eyes stared vacantly, and the usually dapper writer was decked out in shabby clothes that were unlikely even his own. Moran, meanwhile, kept Poe in that part of the hospital generally reserved for inveterate drunks.

Poe had left Richmond, Virginia, a few days before he was found by Walker, apparently destined for New York. What happened in the intervening period is anyone's guess.

There are no extant medical records related to Poe's end – not even a death certificate – which allows theories about what killed him to abound. Some suggest that he fell victim to some long-standing medical complaint. Others suspect suicide, pointing to his overdosing (possibly accidentally) the previous year on the then-popular painkiller, laudanum. There is also some evidence to suggest that he may have somehow been exposed to poisoning by a heavy metal, such as lead or mercury. Edwin J. Barton, meanwhile, used his book *Midnight Dreary: The Mysterious Death of Edgar Allan Poe* to explain how he was downed by a murderous conspiracy related to his personal life.

However, there is a widely held view that Poe died as the result of alcohol abuse. Part of the challenge in trying to establish the truth at this late stage is that Snodgrass and Moran both proved notably unreliable witnesses. Moran puffed up his version of events to suit the audience he was addressing at any given moment. For instance, he initially reported Poe's dying words as 'Lord, help my poor soul' but would later claim that Poe had actually said: 'The arched heavens encompass me, and God has his decree legibly written upon the frontlets of every created human being, and demons incarnate, their goal will be the seething waves of blank despair.' A suitably poetic last offering maybe, but one that does rather stretch credibility.

Snodgrass was little better, claiming Walker's initial letter had described Poe as 'in a state of beastly intoxication' (it did not). Snodgrass was a great supporter of the temperance movement, and it served his political ends to show how even a figure as celebrated as Poe could be brought low by evil liquor. The idea that Poe had succumbed to the devil drink was also propagated by the murky figure of Rufus Wilmot Griswold, a professional rival who somehow managed to become the executor of Poe's literary estate. His duplicitousness is evident from an anonymous obituary he wrote portraying Poe as a wretched old soak, which he followed with a biography peddling a similar line (with added drug addictions). Although Poe's true friends strongly questioned Griswold's assertions, this dismal piece of character assassination was all too readily accepted as fact.

Yet there is another theory that, fanciful as it sounds at first, might hold the truth. At the time Poe was in Baltimore, there were highly contested elections going on. Could Poe have fallen victim to cooping – a ruse in which innocent members of the public were kidnapped, plied with drink or drugs, and then led to a succession of voting booths to make multiple votes in favour of a particular candidate? Such a scam might also explain why Poe was discovered in clothes that were seemingly not his own.

As the odds of establishing Poe's true cause of death lengthen, we are left with a list of possibilities that all too often reflect a third-party agenda. It is only to be hoped that, after offering his public so many delicious puzzles to contend with during his lifetime, Poe would have found some pleasure in being the focal point of such an enduring mystery.

45 MICHAEL FAHERTY – UP IN FLAMES?

It is a familiar plot device in film and fiction, but debate has long raged over whether spontaneous human combustion really exists or not. So when a coroner in modern-day Ireland declared that 76-year-old Michael Faherty had been killed as a result of it, there were gasps of disbelief around the world. Critics rounded on the verdict, but is mainstream science justified in dismissing the judgment?

It was early morning, a few days before Christmas 2010, when a neighbour of Mr Faherty in Ballybane, Galway, awoke to the sound of a smoke alarm. Seeing smoke billowing from Faherty's house, he immediately sought the aid of the emergency services. When the fire brigade broke into the property, they were met with a sorrowful sight. Mr Faherty lay dead on his living-room floor, his body badly burnt.

Yet mixed in with the sense of tragedy was a feeling of utter puzzlement. The property itself bore hardly any signs of fire damage, save for the floor on which the body lay and the ceiling above. Furthermore, after a thorough inspection of the building, the fire brigade found no evidence of any accelerants, and nothing to lead them to think that Faherty had been a victim of foul play. It is true that the corpse lay close to an open fire, but investigators were satisfied that this was not the cause of the fatal blaze either.

An inquest into the death convened in September 2011 under the guidance of the coroner for West Galway, Dr Ciaran McLoughlin. Having pored over expert testimony and assorted academic texts, he reached an astounding conclusion: 'This fire was thoroughly investigated and I'm left with the conclusion that this fits into the category of spontaneous human combustion, for which there is no adequate explanation.' In his 25 years of experience, he had never recorded a verdict like it.

So what is spontaneous human combustion? In short, it is an event where a person bursts into flames despite the apparent absence of an external heat source. The first recorded episode dates to 1663 when a Parisian woman was said to have gone up in smoke, even while the straw bed on which she was sleeping remained intact. However, many within the scientific community consider the idea of spontaneous human combustion as nothing more than hokum.

One alternative theory is that victims succumb to what is known as the 'wick effect'. In these cases, it is argued, a heat source (such as a cinder or cigarette ash) sets the victim's clothing alight. At the same time, somewhat gruesomely, the skin splits to expose fatty deposits, so that the clothing acts as a wick and the fat as candle wax. In this way, the fire burns as long as there is fat to feed it, but then dies out, leaving the surrounding environment untainted. That's all well and good, except that some alleged cases of spontaneous human combustion involve victims whose internal organs show no signs of fire damage.

Furthermore, in the case of Michael Faherty the coroner explicitly ruled out the fireplace as the source of the blaze, and there were no reported alternative heat sources. And while spontaneous human combustion is by no means a commonly reported phenomenon, it is not without precedent. There have been about 200 reported cases in the last three centuries, from all corners of the globe. An American, Frank Baker, is one of a very rare group who claim to have survived an episode. According to Baker, he was preparing to go on a fishing trip with a friend in the mid-1980s when, while sitting on a sofa, he suddenly went up in flames. He relates that, as the flames engulfed him, he and his friend were able to smother them before they could do too much lasting damage. His doctor allegedly told him that the fire had 'burned from the inside out'.

It is a characteristic of humanity that we fear death – our powerlessness to ultimately evade it, its unpredictability and sometimes seeming randomness. For many, the idea of death by spontaneous combustion is about as bad as it gets. It also fits the bill for the kind of death that science does not much like – one that may not be rationalized and thus countered. But surely it is folly to believe that something does not exist simply because science is yet to understand it?

46 THE 'BOY IN THE BOX'

Few stories in this book are more tragic than that of Philadelphia's 'Boy in the Box' – the body of a young child, found discarded in an old cardboard box in the city during the 1950s. No one fitting the victim's description was ever reported missing, nor was anyone ever called to account for his demise. To this day, the child's identity is officially unknown, an enduring blight on the conscience of modern America.

In late February 1957, a man walking in Philadelphia's Fox Chase area spotted a box. Inside, wrapped in a blanket, was the badly bruised, naked corpse of a child. Experts put his age at between three and six years. Curiously, his nails had been trimmed and his hair inexpertly cut. An autopsy determined he died as a result of blows to the head. The case garnered much publicity, but efforts to establish the child's identity met with a singular lack of success. Missing-person records were checked, but there was no trace of a report that might correspond to the infant. Extensive investigations at orphanages proved similarly fruitless.

Lists of possible suspects – violent drifters, known child-abusers, and even a mother who had previously disposed of her daughter's corpse in a bin – were looked into, but nothing stuck. There was for a time a theory (supported by testimony from a psychic brought in on the case) that the answer lay at a local foster home, but the investigator who pursued this line most energetically (one Remington Bristow of the medical examiner's office) died in the early 1990s, having been unable to find any clinching evidence.

In 2002, it was reported that a psychiatrist from Ohio had contacted the police in Philadelphia. She had a client (known only as 'M') who claimed her parents had bought a boy in the mid-1950s for the purpose of sexual abuse. One day M's mother had beaten the child, apparently known as Jonathan, to death. The following day she had driven with the then-ten-year-old M to a remote road, where the two of them disposed of the body. M said that a passing motorist had stopped to see if they needed help, believing they were suffering car trouble. Despite concerns about M's reliability, the account tallies intriguingly with a witness report taken back in 1957.

So it may be that we at last know the circumstances surrounding the death of the 'Boy in the Box', yet the true identities of the child and those responsible for his murder remain unknown, protected by impenetrable client confidentiality.

47 WHO WAS JACK THE RIPPER?

He is surely the most infamous murderer in the annals of British crime, yet over 125 years since he wrought his reign of terror over London, the identity of Jack the Ripper remains a mystery. Dozens of suspects have been proposed, spanning the entire class structure, amid allegations of cover-ups at the highest levels of society. But even modern technology cannot provide us with conclusive proof of the killer's identity.

The air of decorum we tend to associate with 'Victorian England' was shattered in 1888 when a serial killer began going about his brutal work in Whitechapel, an insalubrious neighbourhood in London's East End. The first commonly accepted murder was that of prostitute Mary Ann Nichols at the end of August. There were a further four 'canonical' murders (i.e. attacks generally agreed to be the work of the Ripper), with each of the victims a prostitute. They were: Annie Chapman (killed on 8 September), Elizabeth Stride and Catherine Eddowes (both killed on 30 September) and Mary Jane Kelly (killed 9 November). Six more killings, pre- and post-dating these, are often linked to the Ripper, though his culpability is disputed.

The Ripper dispatched his victims with a knife, and in four of the five 'canonical' cases (the exception being Elizabeth Stride), the bodies were grossly mutilated. Such was the knife-work and apparent anatomical knowledge involved that police assumed the culprit was most likely a trained medical man or a butcher. Yet, despite public pressure for an arrest, no one was brought to justice.

The search for the killer has supported a booming industry ever since. Upwards of 100 suspects have been scrutinized – some highly credible, and others fantastical to say the least. For instance, few now give much credence to the once-popular theory that the assailant was Queen Victoria's grandson – Albert Victor, Duke of Clarence – driven mad by syphilis. We may also be reasonably sceptical that there was a conspiracy involving, variously, the royal family, the police, the Freemasons and Lord Salisbury (the then-Prime Minister) as they attempted to cover up the existence of a love child fathered by Albert Victor to a lowly shop girl. Another suspect with royal connections was the Queen's obstetrician, Sir John Williams, who has been accused of the killings for the purposes of scientific research, despite a lack of hard evidence.

A further 'celebrity' suspect is the painter Walter Sickert, some of whose grimly evocative works have been critiqued as renderings of Ripper crime scenes. Crime writer Patricia Cornwell is a particularly strong advocate of his guilt, but few other serious 'Ripper-ologists' give much weight to the supposition.

We do know the police discovered and then removed graffiti close to the Eddowes murder scene that read 'The Juwes [sic] are not the men to be blamed for nothing'. Fearing the daub might spark an anti-Semitic backlash, senior officers decided to get rid of what some believe may have been crucial evidence. Others, though, believe the slogan was painted merely to misdirect. The crimes certainly attracted more than their fair share of hoaxers, with a number of letters purporting to be from the killer proving particularly unhelpful.

Nonetheless, there are those who remain convinced that some of these letters were genuine, leading to the shocking suggestion that we should actually be looking for Jill the Ripper. In the mid-2000s, an Australian academic called Ian Findlay carried out DNA tests on several items of correspondence deemed most likely to be genuine, and determined that their author may have been a woman. It was a notion backed up by author John Morris in his book *Jack the Ripper: The Hand of a Woman*, who pointed the finger at Lizzie Williams, wife of the aforementioned Sir John.

A motley assortment of other shady characters have their accusers too. In 2014, DNA analysis of a shawl that may (or may not) have been found at the scene of the Eddowes killing and may (or may not) have belonged to the victim, produced a connection to one Aaron Kosminski, a Polish Jewish immigrant who had witnessed terrible atrocities as a child in the Russian empire at a time of anti-Jewish pogroms. He suffered severe mental trauma and was institutionalized after coming to the attention of police in connection with the Ripper murders. Nonetheless, DNA analysis of a disputed piece of evidence cannot be considered conclusive. While Kosminski must remain in the frame, it is certainly not 'Case Closed'.

Whoever was responsible for these grotesque crimes was by definition a mad man (or even mad woman) but retained the mental faculties to expertly hide their identity. Whether they were assisted in this by an elevated position in society, we may never know.

48 THE DEATH OF LEE HARVEY OSWALD

The assassination of President John F. Kennedy on 22 November 1963 left a deep scar on the American psyche. It has also attracted more conspiracy theories than perhaps any crime in history. Lee Harvey Oswald was apprehended for the murder within hours: as he was being moved under police escort the following day, Dallas club-owner Jack Ruby emerged from the shadows to shoot him – but why?

Oswald was initially depicted as a lone-wolf communist sympathizer, but it is now widely accepted that there was a conspiracy to shoot the President. Some say it was disgruntled Cuban dissidents. Others accuse right-wingers with a grudge or point the finger at the secret services. Alternatively, it was mobsters fearing a White House clampdown. Amid all this conjecture stands the curious figure of Jack Ruby, who killed Oswald in front of a television audience of millions. Was Ruby, as he sometimes claimed, driven by grief at the loss of Kennedy, along with a desire to show that 'Jews had guts' and save Jackie Kennedy the pain of Oswald's trial?

There are many who refuse to accept that he was simply a loose cannon who seized his moment to take vengeance on the most infamous man in America. True, the 52-year-old Ruby had a family history of mental illness and was himself prone to bouts of sudden violence that he subsequently seemed to forget. He also customarily carried a gun, as he was often transporting large amounts of cash from his night-club. But are these details all just a little too convenient?

Ruby was, after all, a career criminal with links to organized crime – did the Mob kill Kennedy in response to his administration's clampdown on underworld activities? Some have argued Ruby was too unreliable to be trusted with the job of dispatching Oswald. But did his mobster associates believe Ruby could manipulate his local police connections to engineer the attack? Or was he forced into the deed to pay off a debt?

Ruby died of cancer in 1967, while fighting his 1964 murder conviction. In a televised interview in 1965, he said: 'Everything pertaining to what's happening has never come to the surface. The world will never know the true facts of what occurred, my motives. The people who had so much to gain, and had such an ulterior motive for putting me in the position I'm in, will never let the true facts come above board to the world.'

49 ALFRED LOEWENSTEIN

Alfred Loewenstein was for a while known as the richest man in the world. He was also ruthless and had many enemies. On 4 July 1928, as he crossed the English Channel in his private aircraft, he went to use the facilities – minutes later he was found missing, with one of the plane doors open. His body was discovered 15 days later – was it suicide, a cruel accident or something more untoward?

Born in Belgium in 1877, Loewenstein came to London during the First World War and became hugely wealthy playing the markets. Various critics accused him of criminality, arrogance and an utter lack of ethics but, whatever the truth, he accumulated a fortune worth around US$12 million at 1920s' prices. He used some of this to satisfy his lust for the finer things. He was aboard his personal plane – one of the first with an on-board toilet – flying from Croydon (near London) to Brussels when nature called, and he headed for the plane's bathroom, accessed at the rear of the cabin via one of two doors (the other door was the main entrance/exit).

When he did not reappear after some minutes, his secretary went to investigate and found the bathroom empty but the main door flapping open. Assuming Loewenstein had plunged to his death after becoming confused as to which door was which (associates confirmed he was increasingly absent-minded), the secretary related his sad discovery to his fellow flyers – the pilot, a mechanic, a valet and two lady stenographers. The plane landed on a deserted beach in Normandy, remaining there for half an hour for reasons that remain unclear. It then made for a nearby airfield to report what had happened. Loewenstein's body was eventually found off Boulogne on 19 July.

News of his death caused a temporary market crash, and the rumour mill went into overdrive. The British Air Ministry seemed to rule out accidental death by concluding the main door could not be inadvertently opened at flying altitude. Inevitably, some suspected his staff of killing him (possibly in collusion with family members), using the lost half hour on the Normandy beach to cover their tracks. Others alleged suicide, citing the diminishing fortunes of his company or impending revelations of corruption. Curiously, Loewenstein's wife did not attend his funeral, where he was buried in an unmarked grave. Was this evidence, some wondered, that his death was faked? If you're the richest man in the world, perhaps nothing is impossible.

50 THE ASSASSINATION OF OLOF PALME

Sweden has a reputation as an affluent, confident and peaceable country, so it was all the more shocking when its Prime Minister, Olof Palme, was gunned down on a Stockholm street in 1986. The one man convicted was later acquitted on appeal, and there remains a multitude of theories as to who wanted Palme dead and why, with blame directed as far afield as Eastern Europe, South America, Africa and Asia.

It was late on 28 February 1986 when Palme and his wife, Lisbet, were wandering through the centre of the Swedish capital after a night at the cinema. A man who prided himself on maintaining a degree of normality, Palme had refused the protection of bodyguards. Out of nowhere, a lone assailant appeared, fatally shooting Palme at close range and firing a second shot that wounded Lisbet. As members of the public raised the alarm and tried to save the Prime Minister, the attacker fled on foot.

Some 25 witnesses gave statements to the police, but none had seen the assassin close-up. Most described a man aged between 30 and 50, around 1.8 metres (6 ft) tall, wearing a dark jacket and with a distinctive walk, possibly caused by a limp. The murder weapon is believed to have been a Smith & Wesson revolver – one was recovered from a lake in Dalarna, Central Sweden, in 2006 and while there is significant circumstantial evidence to suggest it was the weapon used, its years in the water meant that forensic scientists were unable to confirm the fact.

In 1988, police arrested a career criminal called Christer Pettersson, whose long list of convictions included manslaughter in the 1970s. He was identified by Lisbet Palme as the shooter, duly convicted and sentenced to life imprisonment. However, he was acquitted on appeal in 1989, with the High Court citing problems in the organization of the identity parade, the absence of a murder weapon and the lack of motive.

Pettersson died in 2004, and two years later a television documentary team interviewed some of his known associates who claimed he had admitted his guilt. His intended target, they said, had been a drug dealer known to inhabit the area in which the shooting took place, who bore a striking resemblance to Palme. Though others have since doubted this witness testimony, it could just be that the most high-profile crime in Swedish history was a case of mistaken identity.

Other investigators, though, remain convinced that Palme was the victim of a conspiracy. In an age when the right-of-centre politics of Reagan and Thatcher were coming to the fore, Palme and his Social Democrats remained staunch defenders of the Left. As a keen advocate of civil rights on the international stage, he did not lack enemies either at home or abroad.

Some believe the most likely culprits were domestic right-wing extremists or even a cabal of disgruntled, renegade police officers. It has emerged that Stieg Larsson, who rose to posthumous fame as author of the multi-million-selling Millennium crime novels, studied the case extensively and suggested the murderer was a known right-winger with psychiatric problems and a history of gun use. The suspect he named had indeed been investigated by police, but was found to have a cast-iron alibi. However, the woman who provided him with that alibi subsequently split from him and withdrew her evidence. Nonetheless, no charges have ever been brought against the suspect.

Another theory has it that Palme was killed by assassins run by the Yugoslav secret services, who planned to frame right-wing Croatian separatists. Others, meanwhile, have attempted to pin the blame on Kurdish dissidents. Then there is a version of events in which Palme stumbled upon evidence that a huge deal negotiated between a leading Swedish arms manufacturer and the Indian government had been secured with bribes. Was he killed before he could pull the plug on the deal?

However, in the view of many commentators, a South African connection offers the most convincing of the many conspiracy theories. Only a week before his death, Palme had addressed an anti-apartheid meeting and called for the elimination of the apartheid system. Sweden, meanwhile, had donated significant funds to Nelson Mandela's African National Congress and there were rumours that his administration had channelled funds from Moscow too. Addressing South Africa's post-apartheid Truth and Reconciliation Committee in 1996, a former senior police officer, Colonel Eugene de Kock, claimed that Palme had been the target of a government-sponsored assassination squad. His version of events was backed up by other leading figures from the police force of that era, although there was some disagreement as to the precise identity of the assassin.

51 ROBERTO CALVI – GOD'S BANKER

Roberto Calvi was the boss of one of Italy's biggest banks, and mixed with many of the most powerful people in the country. Yet his death was a pitiful one – his body was found hanging beneath London's Blackfriars Bridge one bleak morning in 1982. Suicide or murder? There was, it soon became clear, no shortage of people who might want him dead, but the full truth of what befell him remains hidden.

Roberto Calvi was chairman of Banco Ambrosiano, the second-largest privately owned bank in Italy. It was a post that saw him embroiled in scandal and contro-versy long before his death. In 1978, a currency export scam had seen the venerable institution become subject of a crim-inal investigation, and in 1981 Calvi was convicted for his role in the scheme, receiving a four-year suspended sentence and a fine equivalent to several million dollars. Yet while his appeal against the conviction worked its way through the courts, he was allowed to retain his position with the bank.

Calvi, though, knew better than anyone that the bank's prospects were bleak. In fact, it was running on borrowed time. In early June 1982, he wrote to Pope John Paul II personally (the Vatican Bank was the largest single share-holder in Banco Ambrosiano, hence Calvi's nickname of 'God's banker'). Calvi realized his bank was trapped in debt from which it could not recover – some estimate that it had liabilities of some US$1.5 billion. He warned the Pope that its eventual collapse would likely see the Catholic Church 'suffer the gravest damage'.

On 10 June 1982, a few days after writing this letter, Calvi fled Italy using a false passport. It is believed he went to Switzerland, from where he hired a private plane to fly him to London. It was around 7.30 a.m. on 18 June that a postal worker discovered his body hanging from scaffolding underneath Blackfriars Bridge. His clothing had been weighted with bricks, and his pockets were stuffed with cash to the value of $15,000.

In July 1982, an inquest held in the UK returned a verdict of suicide, but Calvi's family were not convinced. A second inquest a year later recorded an open verdict, stating that the exact cause of death had not been established. The Calvi family, convinced that Roberto had been murdered, paid for a further private investigation in the 1990s, including an exhumation. Cutting-edge forensic techniques showed that Calvi's shoes had no signs of the paint and rust one would have expected to see if he had climbed the scaffold and hanged himself. It also became apparent that the river tides on the morning his corpse was found would have permitted someone to suspend him from the scaffolding while standing on a boat. Furthermore, there was also no sign that Calvi had touched the bricks found stuffed in his pockets, and wounds on his neck were not consistent with hanging.

It was beginning to look very much like a murder, and one committed before his body was hanged. But who might have had reason to do it? It might actually have been quicker to list those who had no motive. Many prominent figures within Italy's organized-crime scene lost money in the collapse of

Banco Ambrosiano. Then there was the Vatican link – what was the 'gravest damage' that imperilled the Holy See? Just how much had the Vatican Bank known of its subsidiary's clandestine operations? In 1984, the Vatican Bank paid a small fortune to more than 100 of Banco Ambrosiano's creditors as a 'recognition of moral involvement'.

It also emerged that Calvi had been a member of the notorious P2 (or Propaganda Due) Masonic lodge. P2 was reputedly packed with influential figures and was said to have been involved in assorted nefarious undertakings while exerting influence at the highest levels of Italian society. Some went so far as to describe it as a 'state within a state'. There has been speculation that Calvi, fearing he was going to be left to take the fall for his bank's collapse, might have threatened to reveal incriminating secrets if old friends did not come to his rescue. In doing so, did he sign his own death warrant? Some have seen masonic symbolism in the placing of the bricks in his clothes and the stuffing of his pockets with cash. It has even been suggested that Blackfriars Bridge was deliberately chosen because P2's members were sometimes known as the *frati neri*, or 'black friars'.

In the years since Calvi's death, various underworld figures have emerged to point the finger at their former partners in crime. In 2005, five organized-crime figures went on trial in Rome for his murder, but in 2007 each was acquitted, with the judge citing insufficient evidence. It seems fair to assume that there are a good number of people still around who know exactly what happened to 'God's banker' but none of them are willing – or able – to talk.

52 THE BORDEN MURDERS

It was the trial that captivated Victorian America: a respectable couple, Andrew and Abby Borden, bludgeoned to death in Fall River, Massachusetts. Their daughter Lizzie, a quiet Sunday School teacher, was accused of the crime. After her acquittal, no one else was ever brought to trial, and Lizzie suffered the opprobrium of her social circle. Did she get away with murder, or was she innocent all along?

On 4 August 1892, the Bordens' maid, Bridget Sullivan, heard Lizzie shouting from the family living room where her father's body lay. He had been hit with an axe 11 times. Upstairs lay Abby's corpse, which had received some 19 blows. It was soon clear to the police that there had been tensions in the household. Lizzie, for instance, rather coolly referred to her stepmother as 'Mrs Borden'. It also emerged that there had been a serious rift with Lizzie and her sister Emma on one side and their father on the other, over property given to members of Abby's family. There had also been a falling-out over some pigeons that Lizzie had cared for but which Andrew had killed.

It was, furthermore, alleged that Lizzie had tried to buy poison the previous day, and a family friend reported that she had discovered Lizzie burning a stained dress on the kitchen grate a few days afterwards. Within a week, Lizzie, who did not help her case with an offhand manner, was arrested. Her trial began three months later.

With only circumstantial evidence to judge, the jury took less than an hour to find Lizzie innocent. But on returning to Fall River, she was ostracized by many former associates convinced of her guilt. One prosecuting lawyer even suggested she had a moral duty to explain how she had got away with it, now that the law could no longer lay its hands on her.

However, her defenders pointed to several other possible killers. Among them was Bridget the maid, who some modern researchers have even suggested was romantically involved with Lizzie. Then there was John Morse, brother of Lizzie's dead mother, who had been staying with the family. Author Arnold Brown, meanwhile, pointed the finger at a disgruntled illegitimate son, while others implicated David Anthony. a suitor of Lizzie's, or even the local doctor, Seabury Bowen, who had seemingly fallen out with the Bordens. Someone clearly got away with murder but it is, perhaps, unfair to assume it was Lizzie.

53 ON THE ZODIAC TRAIL

The Zodiac Killer (or simply 'the Zodiac') is known to have murdered at least five people in hippy-era northern California and attempted to kill two more. Yet in letters to police and media, someone purporting to be the killer claimed to have slaughtered a total of 37. His correspondence sometimes contained cryptograms he said would reveal his identity if solved, but the Zodiac remains uncaptured and the mystery unsolved.

The Zodiac, as he referred to himself in his letters, began his known reign of terror just before Christmas of 1968, when he shot teenage couple Betty Lou Jensen and David Faraday in their car on Lake Herman Road, Benicia. The last murder definitely attributed to him came on 11 October 1969, when he shot 29-year-old taxi driver Paul Stine in San Francisco. In between, he attacked two further couples, using a gun in an assault in Vallejo and a knife during an attack at Lake Berryessa. One partner from each of these couples survived.

Subsequently linked to other slayings from the early 1960s through to the 1970s, the Zodiac phoned in several of his known crimes to the police. He also demanded that newspapers including the *San Francisco Chronicle* and the *San Francisco Examiner* publish a series of notes from him, four of which included codes that would supposedly unmask him. Only one of these has been solved but, alas, turned out merely to be a rant as to the joys of killing. The letters claimed the Zodiac's motivation was to build an army of slaves for the afterlife. As evidence that he was genuine, the author provided crime-scene details that police had not revealed to the public.

Countless suspects have been proposed over the years, usually on the basis of tenuous circumstantial evidence. Arthur Leigh Allen was accused by bestselling writer Robert Graysmith and subsequently investigated by police, but they were unable to establish any forensic link. In 2009, meanwhile, a Californian lawyer called Robert Tarbox claimed he was visited in 1972 by a merchant sailor who said he was the Zodiac and wanted to end his killing spree, but this sailor's identity remains unknown. Then in 2014 one Randy Kenney came forward to report how his friend Louie Myers had confessed to the crimes a year before his 2002 death. Nonetheless, the Zodiac case remains open. If he is not already dead, the murderer will be an old man today, and one, we might guess, who continues to enjoy toying with those he kept in fear for so long.

54 THE SOMERTON MAN

On the evening of 30 November 1948, a couple spotted a well-dressed man lying on Somerton Beach not far from Adelaide. At one point they saw him raise his arm before it fell to the ground. Another couple saw the same figure half an hour later, but he was motionless and they assumed he was asleep. By the next morning he was decidedly dead, from heart failure brought on by suspected poisoning.

The deceased carried no identifying material, but did have a packet of cigarettes that strangely contained a different, more expensive brand. At his inquest, it was suggested that he was the victim of a poison that disappeared from the body very quickly after death – most likely digitalis, perhaps administered via substituted cigarettes.

Then in April 1949, a tiny, rolled-up piece of paper was discovered in a pocket sewn into the waistband of his trousers. It read 'Tamám Shud' ('It is ended') – the last words of a 12th-century Persian text, *The Rubaiyat of Omar Khayyam*. A few months later a man came forward who had found a copy of the relevant edition placed in his unlocked car, which had been parked near to the scene of the death at the relevant time. It was printed by a New Zealand publisher but attempts to trace another copy proved fruitless. At the back of the book was the phone number of a woman local to Somerton Beach called Jessica Thomson. She claimed she had given a copy of *The Rubaiyat* to one Alfred Boxall in 1945, but hopes that the case was cracked, faded when Boxall was tracked down alive and well and still in possession of the aforementioned book.

Also faintly visible in the book were five lines of apparently random letters suggestive of a code, which remains unsolved. The signs pointed to the dead man having been involved in spying, a view given extra credence after Jessica Thomson's daughter reported in 2013 that her mother had lied to the authorities and did know who the dead man was, as did others at 'a level higher than the police force'.

To add to the intrigue, three years prior to Somerton Man's death, one George Marshall was found dead in a Sydney park. With him was a copy of *The Rubaiyat* – purportedly a seventh edition published by Methuen, except that Methuen only published five editions. Was it mere coincidence that at least two men died with editions of Persian texts that didn't really exist? Mrs Thomson and others probably knew, but nobody is telling.

55 THE TRAGEDY AT MAYERLING

On a winter's day in early 1889, a man and woman were found dead in a hunting lodge in woods at Mayerling near Vienna. What turned the tragic scene into a potential scandal with international ramifications was the identity of the victims: Prince Rudolf of Austria, heir to the the Austro-Hungarian Empire, and his 17-year-old lover, Baroness Mary Vetsera. Why did the Habsburg family contrive a cover-up?

Thirty-year-old Rudolf, son of Emperor Franz Josef I of Austria, was unhappily married to Stephanie of Belgium, who reputedly knew of his affair with the young Mary. Rudolf was due to go hunting on 30 January, but when his valet came to rouse him, he found instead the bodies of the prince and his paramour, both dead from gunshot wounds. There was no immediate evidence of third-party involvement. Within hours, Mary's body had been spirited away and buried in secret. When news of a tragedy at the hunting lodge seeped out, only the Prince was reported dead – either from a heart attack, or having been poisoned. Key witnesses, meanwhile, were paid by the imperial household for their silence.

Eventually, and inevitably, news that there had been two victims came to light. Yet still there could be no allegation (in public, at least) that Rudolf had killed his illicit sweetheart.

Equally, suggestions of suicide were clamped down upon, since such a charge would have denied Rudolf a Roman Catholic burial. In the interests of securing his son's after-life, Franz Josef conceded to the Pope that his son had killed himself, but only in a 'deranged state of mind'. Rudolf was duly buried in the family vault, with the Vatican obligingly misplacing records of its own investigation into the affair.

While it is tempting to assume that the two lovers had partaken in a murder–suicide pact (Rudolf was a notoriously mawkish romantic), there are several competing explanations for their demise. There is evidence to suggest only one bullet was fired, with the implication that Mary died by some other means. Did Rudolf strike her dead during a row and, overcome with remorse, take his own life? Might she even have died during a botched abortion? Or was Rudolf an innocent victim himself, either killed by enemies of the state (as his father had suggested), or by malevolent forces within the empire? In his desire to protect his family name, Franz Josef doubtlessly agreed to sacrifice the truth. The chances of it now being recovered from a multilayered web of deceit seem slim.

56 KASPAR HAUSER – MAN OF MYSTERIES

Kaspar Hauser was believed to be aged about 16 when he was found wandering around the centre of Nuremberg in Germany in May 1828. Claiming that he had been raised alone in a small, darkened cell, his true origins have remained a mystery ever since. He died from a stab wound on 17 December 1833, leaving generations to ponder whether he was a lost noble, an incorrigible fantasist or something else entirely.

Hauser arrived at Nuremberg carrying an unsigned letter explaining that he had been in its author's custody since 1812, receiving a rudimentary Christian education but hitherto denied permission to leave his guardian's house. Now, it went on, the boy wished to be a cavalryman as his father had been. A second letter, purportedly from Hauser's mother, gave his name and date of birth (30 April 1812), but both notes were in the same handwriting. Was Hauser himself the author of both?

Over the next few years, he was placed in the care of several individuals. At first it was thought he had been raised semi-wild in nearby forests, but later Hauser claimed his childhood was spent in a tiny darkened cell, where he saw no one save a single occasional visitor who hid his face and taught him basic skills including how to walk, write his name and say 'I want to be a cavalryman, as my father was' in Bavarian. Given this bizarre back story, speculation was intense as to his origins. There was talk that he was an exiled royal – perhaps from the House of Baden or maybe even England or Hungary – but many regarded him simply as an imposter weaving tales to ease his passage through life. Lord Stanhope, a British aristocrat, took particular interest, suspecting Kaspar had Hungarian connections but ultimately concluding that the boy's accounts were untrustworthy.

On 14 December 1833, Hauser received a stab wound to his left breast. He claimed a stranger had attacked him in nearby gardens. In his purse, recovered from the scene, was an enigmatic verse note in mirror-writing that hinted at the assailant's identity. Soon, suspicions grew that the injury was self-inflicted and the note written by the youth himself. Whatever the case, Hauser died that same day. He may have been a swindler or genuinely mentally ill, and just maybe he was even high-born. But whether Kaspar himself knew is debatable. His headstone summed up his life neatly: 'Here lies Kaspar Hauser, riddle of his time. His birth was unknown, his death mysterious. 1833.'

57 ROBERT MAXWELL – ACCIDENT AT SEA?

After escaping Nazi-occupied Czechoslovakia as a young man, Jan Hoch reinvented himself as Robert Maxwell, ascending the ranks of British society to serve as an MP before building a media empire. When he fell to his death while sailing off the Canary Islands, many unanswered questions remained. Had ill health caught up with him, did he commit suicide to avoid impending ruin, or did his enemies get to him first?

By the early 1990s, Maxwell, perhaps best known as the proprietor of Mirror Group Newspapers, headed a house of cards poised to tumble. Post-mortem, it emerged that he had illegally plundered his employees' pension pots in a desperate bid to prop up his empire. His last day, 5 November 1991, was spent aboard his yacht, *Lady Ghislaine*. By nightfall, his body had been discovered floating some 25 kilometres (15 miles) away. Three pathologists failed to agree on a cause of death, but an inquest ruled he had died of a heart attack and accidental drowning. Yet while he suffered serious ill health, many commentators considered this official version of events a little too convenient.

Some suspected he had committed suicide to avoid fraud charges, though few who knew him believed he would be cowed into such action. But we now also know Maxwell was under investigation for alleged war crimes committed during the Second World War. A Jew who lost many family members to the holocaust, he had emerged from the conflict as a decorated hero. All that was now at risk – reason enough to kill himself before the charges could be tested?

Others speculated that he was murdered by foreign agents. Maxwell had long served as a conduit between the Eastern Bloc and Israel, orchestrating complicated deals including arms transfers. He knew things that could embarrass powerful people. Now under threat of trial, might one or more of his international associates have been eager to dispatch him before he could take the witness stand? One take on the story, elucidated by authors Gordon Thomas and Martin Dillon, casts Maxwell as a superspy for the Israeli state. With his finances in disarray, he demanded a huge handout from his Jerusalem paymasters to guarantee his silence. Their response, it is said, was to dispatch crack Mossad agents to kill him.

However he died, Maxwell left behind a tangled web that he and many of those who dealt with him would probably be content to see left unpicked.

STRANGE ENCOUNTERS

58 THE ALIEN AUTOPSY VIDEO

For those convinced that aliens have landed on Earth, 1995 promised to be an *annus mirabilis*, with the release of a video purporting to show a real-life alien autopsy. While the non-believers scoffed, the faithful declared it as irrefutable proof of the legendary Roswell UFO crash of 1947. Although the movie was later confirmed as a hoax, some still contend that the 'real' footage is out there.

The alien autopsy film appeared in a blaze of publicity – there had long been talk that an alien spacecraft had crash-landed at Roswell, New Mexico, in 1947, and that one or more of its inhabitants had been captured by the US government. There was even speculation that the authorities had conducted a full-scale autopsy – and now here, it seemed, was the evidence. What followed was 17 minutes of shadowy, black-and-white footage in which a non-human entity was dissected. Well over a billion people watched the images. Some were utterly convinced that it was genuine, but plenty more remained highly sceptical.

The film's producer and promoter, Ray Santilli, claimed he had stumbled across it in 1992 while on a trip to the United States to buy footage of early rock 'n' roll performers. He alleged a retired military cameraman had offered him 22 reels of footage that he had been harbouring for four decades. Having raised the cash to make the purchase,

Santilli brought the film back to the UK, where he edited it down for public consumption.

In 2006, Santilli admitted that he had in fact created the film with the help of a skilled model-maker and some animal entrails picked up at a local meat market. Yet he refused to describe the film as a fake, instead calling it a 'reconstruction'. He said that the original film had deteriorated so much by the time he bought it that it was unusable. Thus, he said, he set about accurately recreating it, even including a handful of usable frames from the original (though he was unable to specify which ones).

For some, the case was now closed. The film was a categorical fake and Roswell was, after all, fiction. But others refuse to see it in those terms. Santilli might have used up lots of goodwill with his obfuscation, but maybe he was telling the truth about the original footage? Perhaps more pertinently, it has been argued that if the authorities wished to divert attention away from Roswell and human-alien interactions, what more effective way to undermine those trying to shine a light on the episode than by orchestrating an embarrassing 'hoax'?

59 THE MARFA LIGHTS

A few miles east of Marfa in Texas lies an area known as Mitchell Flat. For almost 60 years, and perhaps far longer, it has seen regular reports of an eerie light show of football-sized orbs floating above the ground. Explanations have ranged from alien pyrotechnics and ghostly visitations to peculiar geological and atmospheric conditions. Others, though, believe the truth is to be found on the nearby highway.

It was July 1957's *Coronet Magazine* that first widely publicized the phenomena of the lights, reporting that they appeared up to a couple of dozen nights each year. Witnesses described a range of colours, positions and motion. Sometimes they appeared individually, other times in pairs or larger groups, perhaps just for a moment but occasionally for much longer stretches. What everybody seems to agree upon is that people are seeing something – this is not merely a case of mass hysteria, and indeed, the city has even erected an official viewing platform for its mysterious tourist attraction.

Legend has it that the lights were first witnessed by a local agricultural worker called Robert Reed Ellison way back in 1883. He and fellow settlers suspected that they perhaps emanated from the campfires of the local Native American population. The Native Americans, meanwhile, considered them to be the residue of fallen stars. There have been plenty of other unlikely explanations too, including the suggestion that they are the wandering ghosts of long-fallen Spanish conquistadors.

Others, however, put their faith in more earthbound reasons. The local land is rich in hydrocarbons, so perhaps the lights could result from flammable methane mixing with the air in particular types of weather (just as swamp gas has been known to do). Such conditions might well produce the effect commonly known as 'will-o'-the-wisp' or 'fool's fire', usually seen in marshy areas.

Meanwhile, students from the University of Texas undertook an extensive study that found the lights often corresponded to the movement of car headlights on Route 67. The local area is regularly subject to significant high-low temperature differentials that cause an optical illusion known as 'Fata Morgana'. This, it is claimed, can make simple car lights seem like levitating, glowing orbs. It is certainly a neat solution, but no one knows for sure it is true. So just maybe the lights are the lingering glow of conquistadors' souls after all . . .

60 THE COMTE DE SAINT GERMAIN

In the second half of the 18th century, a mysterious and charismatic figure known as the Comte de Saint Germain swept through the courts of Europe. His origins unclear, he was soon surrounded by myth and legend: some claimed that he could turn base metal into gold, others said he had discovered the secret of eternal life. But just who was this remarkable man . . . and might he still be alive today?

The Comte first came to public recognition in London during the 1740s, where he met, among others, Horace Walpole, son of former Prime Minister Sir Robert Walpole. In a letter to a friend, Horace told of an intriguing figure who would not reveal his real name or from whence he came. Walpole said he was 'odd' and 'mad' but also a virtuoso violin player and accomplished composer who had come to fascinate the Prince of Wales. Meanwhile, allegations that the Comte was on a spying mission went unproven despite his arrest on such charges.

Having come under scrutiny in this way, it was little surprise that Saint Germain drifted away from the London scene, only to turn up a few years later in Paris, wowing the court of Louis XV at Versailles. He was employed by the king to carry out a variety of shady 'diplomatic missions' and was also provided with an extravagantly equipped laboratory where he spent his time working on fabric dyes that he claimed would bring great wealth to the country.

He became a well-known figure in Paris's many salons, celebrated for his sparkling conversation and great intellect. He spoke a vast array of languages and had an encyclopedic knowledge of history. He also famously bestowed diamonds upon acquaintances – a costly pastime for a man with no obvious source of income. Rumours abounded that he could create spectacular gems from a handful of smaller stones. There was also talk (much of it coming from his own mouth) that the Comte was extraordinarily old, with his years countable in centuries rather than decades.

His mystique was only increased by the uncertainty surrounding his origins – questions to which we can still provide only the most uncertain answers. Saint Germain himself sometimes claimed to be the son of a Transylvanian prince, Francis II Rákóczi. According to that particular narrative, he must have been born in the late 1600s, which would have meant that when he was carousing around Europe as a man apparently in his 40s, he was actually in his 60s or 70s. While not an impossibility, it hardly fills one with great faith in the tale. Nonetheless, it is a good deal more convincing than those who claimed he was alive during Christ's lifetime and had, furthermore, attended the Council of Nicaea in AD 325.

Saint Germain later turned up in Russia, where he was implicated in helping Catherine the Great seize the throne. On his travels he crossed paths with the great and good, provoking a spectrum of reactions. Giacomo Casanova, for instance, considered him a 'celebrated and learned imposter', while the great Enlightenment philosopher, Voltaire, called him 'The Wonderman' and described him, with tongue in cheek, as 'a man who never dies, and who knows everything'.

Having supposedly warned Louis XVI and Marie Antoinette of their impending fate at the hands of revolution-aries some years before they succumbed to the guillotine, he turned up in the 1780s in Germany, where he became friends with Prince Charles of Hesse-Cassel. In fact, he ended up living in the Prince's castle and persuaded him to furnish him with yet another laboratory for his now-legendary experiments. It was in this setting that he apparently died at the end of February 1784.

'Apparently', because there were reports that he was seen the following year in the company of the pioneering hypnotist, Anton Mesmer, and the French-born Comtesse d'Adhémar claimed to have spoken with him as late as 1820. Others alleged even later encounters. Members of the Theosophical Society were particularly keen to claim him as one of their own in the late 19th century, while as recently as 1972 a man appeared on French TV ostensibly turning lead into gold in a bid to prove that he was the Comte.

So was Saint Germain a powerful spiritual guru? Or perhaps a sorcerer who had found the elixir of life? Others have gone so far as to suggest he was a time traveller – hence his appearances over a wide span of history, armed with seemingly extraordinary knowledge. Cynics, meanwhile, have him down as a simple fraudster. He was certainly a charismatic figure who knew how to hold the attention of an audience. Spinning yarns when it suited and remaining silent at other times, he died (or did he?) having kept secret both his real identity and the true nature of his capabilities.

61 SPRING-HEELED JACK

It is the very stuff of nightmares: a cloaked figure with inhuman features launching sudden attacks of varying ferocity on innocent victims before leaping his way to escape. In the 19th century, stories of the wicked Spring-Heeled Jack emerged first in London and then up and down the country, while the public struggled to decide if there was a mischievous prankster at large, or if the truth was far less savoury.

The legend of Jack had a low-key beginning in early 1838, when the Lord Mayor of London, Sir John Cowan, announced he had received a letter from someone who referred to themselves only as a 'resident of Peckham'. The correspondent related how he believed some high-born fellows had entered into a dangerous wager encouraging one of their number to commit acts designed to terrorize residents of London and its environs. He was to commit his atrocities in the guise, variously, of a ghost, a bear and the devil himself.

He had, the writer went on, already caused several young women to utterly lose their wits. Furthermore, the story was being covered up, owing to the culprit's illustrious background. In the days following the mayor's address, numerous accounts of strange events and 'wicked pranks' began to circulate, seemingly confirming the 'resident of Peckham's' assertions.

For instance, Mary Stevens, a servant girl, had been walking across Clapham Common the previous October when she was accosted by a curious, dark figure. He proceeded to grab her and tear at her clothes with clammy clawlike fingers until the girl screamed and local residents came to her rescue. Shortly afterwards, a miscreant had jumped out at a coachman close to where Stevens had been attacked, causing his carriage to crash. The ne'er-do-well then leaped to safety over a wall some three metres high, laughing devilishly as he went.

By March 1838, the press had nicknamed the attacker Spring-Heeled Jack. In April came reports of an assault on a man gardening not far from the coastal town of Brighton. This followed hard on the heels, as it were, of reported attacks on two more women, Lucy Scales and Jane Alsop. Alsop had answered the door of the family home to a man claiming to be a policeman. When she followed him as he had requested, he suddenly turned on her, spewing blue and white flames from his mouth. His eyes were, she said, like 'red balls of fire' and he pawed at her with metallic talons. Having screamed and briefly evaded his clutches, she was rescued by her sister – but not before she had received some nasty cuts and grazes to her neck and arms.

Scales, meanwhile, was walking with her sister in London's East End when a figure in a cape jumped out at her. Just as in Alsop's account, he exuded 'blue flame' from his mouth. Miss Scales responded by going into a fit that lasted several hours. The picture was emerging of a tall, thin figure of grotesque appearance, usually wearing a cloak, who specialized in spiteful attacks that left his victims severely distressed. His method of escape always relied, of course, on an ability to jump super-human heights over walls and fences and even across rooftops.

In the years that followed, attacks were regularly reported in locations as widespread as Devon, East Anglia and the Black Country. The last reported incident is generally accepted as having come out of Liverpool in 1904. By then, Spring-Heeled Jack had taken on a folkloric status, and was often invoked by parents in order to inspire obedience in their children.

So what was the truth? Did an incarnation of the devil patrol Queen Victoria's realm? Was this an urban legend turned to mass hysteria? Or did this unpleasant escapade really originate with a group of dissolute young aristocrats who pulled enough well-connected strings to keep their identities secret? (The notoriously roguish Marquess of Waterford, for instance, was long suspected, despite a lack of concrete evidence.)

Whether Jack was myth, practical joker or heinous criminal, it did not stop him from infiltrating the popular imagination and inspiring genuine fear. Take for example the case of Joseph Darby, an unfortunate West Midlands publican who one evening in the 1870s found himself surrounded by police and a baying crowd, sure that they had cornered Spring-Heeled Jack at long last. Joseph was a truly gifted leaper, becoming world champion at the long-defunct sport of spring jumping. He had taken himself off to a local canal, wearing a miner's hat and lamp so he might undertake a little night-time leaping practice. Alas, eagle-eyed locals spotted him and assumed him to be the personification of the fiend who had terrorized Victorian England for so long.

62 *EL CHUPACABRA*

In 1995, news broke from Puerto Rico of large numbers of sheep and goats found dead in mysterious circumstances. The animals reportedly suffered puncture wounds to their chests, and their carcasses were drained of blood. Similar incidents were reported from various corners of South America, as well as the United States. Was this the work of a blood-sucking critter commonly known as *El Chupacabra*?

El Chupacabra (which translates from Spanish as 'goat sucker') might sound like something from a bad 1980s horror flick, but the origins of this purported creature date to March 1995 and the discovery of eight dead sheep in Puerto Rico. Within a few months, the vampiric little monster had been blamed for the deaths of hundreds of farm animals and domestic pets on the island. Initially, there was speculation that a satanic cult was at work, but soon there were eyewitness sightings of the alleged real culprit. Before long, similar reports were received from across North and South America, and even as far away as China.

Those who claim to have seen *El Chupacabra* generally describe a small, stocky creature with a bearlike head and spines running down its back. Its skin is usually described as reptilian in nature – scaly and leathery. It measures up to 1.2 metres (4 ft) tall and stands on its hind legs or hops in the style of a kangaroo. To put it mildly, it looks other-worldly.

A few initial reports soon turned into a flood as the story took on a life of its own. Soon there were even photographs and video footage purportedly showing the demon killer. Yet most of this evidence could be quickly discounted, typically showing instead animals such as raccoons, wild dogs, coyotes or foxes suffering from mange. This condition rendered the creatures hairless and gave them a distinct 'not of this Earth' appearance. It was even suggested that the very first eyewitness report had been influenced (perhaps unconsciously) by images of the creature Sil from the science-fiction horror movie *Species* that was released the same year.

While it is clear that there is no vast army of creatures roaming around the Americas and southern Asia sucking the blood of livestock, there is still a mystery of what happened in those few genuine cases where animals were found drained of their life blood. Was this all the work of mad-eyed mangy dogs, or might there be some genetic mutant at work that no one wants to acknowledge? The idea of *El Chupacabra* is easy to ridicule but does it perhaps hide a darker truth?

63 WHO ARE THE MEN IN BLACK?

Before Will Smith and Tommy Lee Jones made them cool in the hugely successful *Men in Black* film franchise, talk of MIB (as they are often called) would likely have left you with an uneasy feeling. Since the late 1940s, rumours have circulated of shadowy figures delivering veiled threats to those with the audacity to talk publicly about the existence of UFOs. But if they do exist, just who are the MIB?

Eyewitnesses usually describe the MIB as dressed in all-black suits and often wearing sunglasses. One suspects they would cut quite dashing figures, if only they weren't so intimidating. Their primary role, according to those who claim to have encountered them, is to dissuade witnesses of UFO phenomena from digging too deep.

This has led to much speculation as to whom the MIB report. For some, the answer is simple: these are government employees charged with making sure that ordinary citizens do not get wind of the terrible extraterrestrial secrets held by the state. Others, though, have pondered whether we are dealing with a different sort of organization altogether – one that wields far more power than a mere national government. Some have even wondered whether the MIB aren't themselves alien life forms, keen to stop interfering humans getting in the way of their intergalactic enterprises.

The earliest reports of MIB seem to date to around

1947. That year, for instance, a Washington State harbour patrolman called Harold Dahl claimed that he had received a visit after reporting a 'UFO crash' on Maury Island in Puget Sound. In 1953, meanwhile, Connecticut resident and proprietor of the International Flying Saucer Bureau, Albert Bender, said he had been terrified into giving up his investigations (and publication of an associated magazine) after a visit from three characters in dark suits.

While critics suggested this was all a tall tale concocted to hide the fact that Bender was quitting due to financial losses, his friends implied that the MIB had possible associations with the White House or the secret services. However, as time went by Bender himself painted a different picture. He authored a book in which he suggested the MIB were actually of supernatural origin.

By then, Men in Black had become a part of the cultural mainstream, typically depicted in groups of two or three and driving stylish cars such as Cadillacs. In witness accounts, their behaviour ranges from the distinctly odd to the outright menacing, but always with the aim of putting off those who are getting too close to the truth of a UFO mystery. It is, some might argue, comic-book stuff that does little for the credibility of the UFO movement. Certainly, there is an army of cynics who believe that MIB are figments of the same imaginations that conceive skies full of UFOs and little green men secretly running our planet.

However, it's possible the MIB do exist – just not quite in the form that some would have you believe. There is growing support for the theory that the MIB legend is part of a hugely complex web of deceit operated by the government in Washington over a period of decades. The real aim, according to this thesis, is not to persuade UFOlogists that they should desist in their investigations. Instead, it is to create another layer of UFO folklore. By suggesting that there really is something to hide, the argument goes, the government hopes to encourage widespread belief in aliens and flying saucers, the better to distract attention from the real 'truth' behind most UFO sightings (i.e. the testing of advanced weapons and defence technology).

If that sounds like unidentified pie in the sky, consider the testimony of Richard Doty, who says that he was a US Air Force special investigations officer charged with going undercover among the UFO fraternity to just this end during the 1970s and 1980s. Doty claimed to have been involved in the sad case of Paul Bennewitz, a New Mexico technology entrepreneur and UFO enthusiast who, along with others, witnessed numerous strange light displays in the night sky. Bennewitz became convinced that aliens had reached Earth, and that a malevolent species was operating out of the so-called Dulce Base in New Mexico, experimenting on humans and conducting mind-control research with the cooperation of the White House. Increasingly regarded as a crank, his mental health went into steep decline. It is now widely accepted that there was a conspiracy to supply Bennewitz with misinformation so that he might discredit himself – and, some have argued, to divert attention from covert activities at the nearby Kirtland Air Force Base, the possible true source of the original light shows. So maybe the MIB don't just belong to comic books or the movies – but their goals may not be quite so obvious as they seem.

64 THE MYSTERY OF MERCY BROWN

It is a scene that reads as if it has been lifted from the pages of Bram Stoker. In a Rhode Island graveyard in the late 19th century, a young woman's coffin is opened. Those present are appalled to find that the two-month-buried body remains in a state of non-decomposition. They conclude that the girl, Mercy Brown, is a vampire and, moreover, is draining the lifeblood of her brother. But what was really going on?

Had all been well, it is likely that the Brown family of Rhode Island would mean little to anybody today. An ordinary, middling sort of couple, George and Mary Brown moved to the town of Exeter in the 1870s when their children were young. But the 1880s brought them tragedy upon tragedy. First, Mary fell ill with tuberculosis (also known as consumption) – the awful wasting disease that claimed so many lives in the era – and after a rapid decline, she died.

The same fate soon befell her eldest daughter, Mary Olive, who succumbed in 1888. Two years later, the son, Edwin, fell ill with the same complaint. Against the odds, though, he fought for his life long and hard. In fact, while he struggled on, his younger sister, Mercy, caught the disease and perished in January 1892. Having witnessed the cruel decimation of his family, George Brown was understandably desperate to do whatever he could to save his son.

Although New England was a most civilized part of the world at the end of the 19th century, it had a long reputation for superstition dating back to the 17th-century Salem Witch Trials. With scientific knowledge of tuberculosis limited, its symptoms – including severe weight loss – were sometimes interpreted as signs that the very life of a sufferer was being sucked out of them by some malevolent force. Given that the Browns had endured more than their fair share of heartache, it was suggested that perhaps there was a sinister spirit at work within the family.

So it was that George Brown agreed in March to have the bodies of his wife and two daughters exhumed. Mary and Mary Olive were recovered first and showed all the normal signs of decomposition. But when Mercy's body was brought to light, it did not. The flesh was well preserved, while her hair and fingernails seemed to have actually grown. Liquid blood was recovered from the body too. Furthermore, there was speculation that the corpse was found in a different position to the one in which it had been lain two months earlier. For good measure, a few locals now piped up to say they had seen her spirit stalking the graveyard.

With Mercy thus having been identified as a life-sucking vampire, her heart was removed forthwith, before being burnt on a stone. Even more bizarrely, the ashes were then mixed into a drink that was fed to Edwin. Perhaps unsurprisingly to modern eyes, this had little effect, and within two months Edwin too was dead. So had George Brown spawned a demonic daughter who cheated death by feasting on the life force of her immediate family? This was the conclusion to which many jumped. Even today, there are those who point to Mercy Brown as evidence that vampires exist outside mere folklore.

Certainly, the circumstances of her cadaver as they were related were peculiar. However, science offers credible explanations for all the curious features. It being deep winter when she died, the ground had been too frosty to dig her grave, so she was stored in a crypt above ground, awaiting later interment. It was, in effect, like being held in a cold store, hence the well-preserved nature of her flesh.

As for her blood, it is quite possible that it coagulated in her heart and liver only to liquefy again at a later stage. Then we come to the supposedly growing hair and fingernails, though this was almost certainly not the case. Rather, cells dehydrate post-mortem causing the skin to shrink and tighten, which can make hair and nails seem to protrude more than in life. And what of the alleged movement of the corpse? It has been reliably reported that non-embalmed bodies may sit up, jolt and even emit groans as the early stages of decomposition set in.

So was Mercy Brown a malevolent spirit? That is what some would have you believe, and there is little to be offered in the way of physical evidence to persuade them otherwise. But Mercy Brown was surely a victim herself. First of family tragedy, then of a brutal disease that stole her own young life away and, finally, of superstition and innuendo. Whatever the causes of the non-decomposition of Mercy Brown, she surely deserves the sympathy of the living, rather than their suspicion and loathing.

65 THE MOTHMAN

The Mothman has achieved legendary status through depictions in print and on screen. Yet this urban myth has its roots in a number of apparently genuine sightings reported over the course of 12 months in West Virginia. Was it an instance of mass hysteria or the work of an extreme practical joker? Or was there really a creature of unknown origin whose appearance seemed to forewarn of impending doom?

The tale begins on 12 November 1966 in the town of Clendenin, West Virginia, when a team of labourers digging in a cemetery reported seeing a human-like winged figure fly out of a tree and over their heads. Three days later at Point Pleasant, a city in nearby Mason County, two couples filed a report with police saying they had seen a large, white creature with wings spanning several metres and eyes that glowed red. This devilish incarnation appeared as they were driving near a former Second World War munitions plant.

Over the following weeks, more sightings rolled in. Some were undoubted hoaxes – a gang of construction workers, for instance, admitted tying red flashlights to helium balloons in a bid to terrify passers-by. But many reports were made in good faith – the sense of bewilderment was summed up by a local newspaper headline: 'Couples See Man-Sized Bird . . . Creature . . . Something'.

Then, on 15 December 1967, the Silver Bridge, a suspension bridge over the Ohio River between Point Pleasant and Galipolis, Ohio, collapsed, killing 46 people. After the tragedy, the rush of Mothman sightings dried up, and although the collapse was blamed on metal fatigue, some locals started to make a link between the Mothman and the accident. A few claimed the strange, winged figure was responsible, while others suggested it was merely a harbinger of terrible things.

Today, Point Pleasant is home to a Mothman Museum and hosts an annual Festival – the legend is big business for the city. Sceptics might suggest that the story has been perpetuated for cold economic reasons, and at the time of the initial sightings, officials claimed people had merely seen a large heron, crane or owl. Others, meanwhile, pointed to a supernatural origin or suggested that there was a mutant animal at large, perhaps somehow linked to the former munitions plant. Something was loose in West Virginia in the late sixties – perhaps the imaginations of the locals, but just maybe something more sinister.

66 THE *FLYING DUTCHMAN*

The legend of the *Flying Dutchman* – a spectral ship fated to sail the seas for all eternity – is nothing more than that, is it? A myth conjured up in the minds of old sea dogs, designed to entertain and terrify in equal measure. But is it possible that the story is rooted in fact? And if it is pure fiction, why were there reported sightings of the vessel all the way into the 20th century?

So infamous is the tale of the *Flying Dutchman* that the name has become a generic term for any 'ghost ship'. In probably the earliest rendering of the story, dating to the end of the 18th century, *Flying Dutchman* was not the given name of a particular ship, but referred to a Dutch man-of-war, captained by one Phillip Vanderdecken, that was apparently wrecked in a storm off Africa's Cape of Good Hope in the second half of the 1600s. Before long, sailors returning to Europe claimed to have seen the ship and her crew riding on the ocean wave in ghostly form. Cynics say these witnesses had fallen foul of some optical illusion or that long periods on perilous seas caused their minds to play cruel tricks. In other words, this was a case of mass hysteria.

Yet for all that, new sightings of the *Flying Dutchman* continued over the ensuing decades and centuries. Sometimes, the ship seemed to be careering towards the reporting vessel, only to disappear just as a collision seemed inevitable.

Perhaps most famously, the fabled boat was allegedly sighted by several crew members aboard the British naval ship, HMS *Bacchante*, in 1881. This testimony was particularly valued since one of them was the Prince of Wales (later King George V). Another British naval crew documented a new sighting some 40 years later and there was a spate of further encounters reported by British and German vessels active in the area during the Second World War.

Of course, the idea of a ship crewed by ghoulish figures and doomed to sail for evermore is hard to swallow outside of a novel or movie. Nonetheless, we are left with a crowded roll call of those who claim to have seen the *Flying Dutchman* over more than three centuries. Could they all be part of an elaborate hoax? Or else have they all succumbed to the same strange form of hysteria? If we accept that these witnesses, many of them characters toughened by years at sea themselves, are seeing something out of the ordinary, why has no one been able to satisfactorily explain what it is?

67 THE COLARES ISLAND UFO
    WAVE

In late 1977, there was a spate of reported sightings of unidentified flying objects over the city of Colares in northern Brazil's
Pará state. Some claim tens and possibly hundreds of incidents
were logged, with witnesses reporting accompanying injuries,
including blood loss. The Brazilian Air Force is said to have
been involved in an operation to restore order – did they find
proof of an alien assault?

Many of those reporting sightings provided similar
narratives: in most cases, an object (or objects) emit-
ting bright light was seen flying at low altitude, its
light causing physical symptoms ranging from dizziness and
shivering to scarring. These scars, allegedly accompanied
by corresponding blood loss, led to the objects being nicknamed *chupa-chupa* (literally, 'the Sucker'). As a climate
of hysteria grew, the local mayor apparently turned to the
Air Force in the hope of returning order to his beleaguered
town. UFOlogists report that the resulting intervention was
designated *Operação Prato* ('Operation Saucer') and carried
on into 1978. During the few months that it lasted, Air
Force personnel supposedly gathered pictorial evidence of
the strange phenomena while simultaneously restoring calm
to the area. The number of sightings gradually dwindled and
the operation was allegedly ended without notice.

In the late 1990s, someone claiming to be a senior officer involved in Operation Saucer gave an interview to researchers in which he recounted day-to-day aspects of the mission. Within three months he was found dead, having apparently hanged himself. Although his interview had not been particularly revelatory, his sad demise inevitably led some commentators to wonder whether there had been a concerted attempt to make sure he kept his silence in future.

Those who claim to have encountered the UFOs continue to debate whether their uninvited visitors were intent on harming those on the ground or were simply partaking in an information-gathering exercise. Others suggest that Colares merely fell victim to an unexplained dose of mass hysteria. Alternatively, were the UFOs the product of some Earth-bound technological innovation that the authorities wished to test but did not want to discuss in public? With the Brazilian Air Force reputedly reluctant to release their files on the alleged incident (which some say run to hundreds of pages), the speculation as to what happened at Colares is set to continue.

68 A BEAST ON BODMIN MOOR?

Since 1983, there have been at least 60 reported sightings in England's West Country of a large, catlike animal of a type not indigenous to the British Isles. Witnesses usually describe a feline somewhere between 90 and 150 centimetres (three to five feet) in length, with white or yellow eyes. The official line is that no such creature exists, but there is a growing body of evidence to suggest that something is out there.

While most sightings have centred on Cornwall's Bodmin Moor, there have been other purported encounters in neighbouring Devon and a number of other rural locations. Occasionally, witnesses have snapped photographs and video footage, some of which is highly persuasive if not conclusive. The best was arguably a 1998 video that seemed to show a large black, panther-like creature. Farmers have reported unexplained livestock mutilations, and by the 1990s there was sufficient hearsay evidence to prompt local MPs to push for an official investigation. The Ministry of Agriculture, Fisheries and Food reported their findings in 1995, concluding that there was no verifiable evidence of big cats at large. Furthermore, it suggested the mutilations were attributable to known indigenous species. But for those convinced that the Ministry had got it wrong, there was a crumb of hope – the authors conceded their inquiry could not categorically disprove the 'big cat' thesis.

Shortly after publication of the report, it looked like the mystery was solved once and for all when a teenage boy recovered an animal skull while out on a riverside walk. The Natural History Museum confirmed that it came from a juvenile leopard, but just when it seemed that the Beast had been found, it was announced that the skull was probably imported as part of a leopard-skin rug.

Sceptics of the Beast narrative point out that the local environment simply cannot sustain a breeding population of such animals. Their opponents, meanwhile, suggest that one or more animals may have escaped from a circus or private collection. An owner lacking the requisite paperwork would doubtless be loath to report such a loss to the authorities. Alternatively, it has been proposed that the Beast is a throw-back to a species once native to the UK, but long thought extinct. In the interests of allaying public fears, the government has good reason to hope the story is mere myth. But while reports of the Beast of Bodmin Moor continue to roll in, there will be many who suspect that the truth has not yet fully emerged.

THE MINNESOTA ICEMAN

In the late 1960s, a Minnesota farmer called Frank Hansen toured fairs and circuses around the country exhibiting a hairy, apelike creature preserved in a block of ice. After a pair of cryptozoologists made the claim that it was an example of a previously unknown hominid species, the creature disappeared from public view for decades. So was the Iceman a classic hoax, or a vital link in our evolutionary development?

ansen claimed he was working at the Arizona State Fair when an enigmatic Californian millionaire told him that, while on a trip overseas, he had bought a strange apelike creature, not dissimilar to popular depictions of Bigfoot. He now wished to put it on display so the public could make up their minds as to what it was. Impressed by Hansen's streak of showmanship, he offered him rights to show the beast for two years. Hansen readily agreed and took possession of the 1.8-metre (6-ft) curiosity.

In 1968, two cryptozoologists (specialists in as-yet-undiscovered animals), Ivan Sanderson and Bernard Heuvelmans, were on the hunt for Bigfoot when they got wind of Hansen's apeman. After a private viewing, they became convinced that they had stumbled upon something extraordinary. Before long, both men had published articles, with Heuvelmans proclaiming a new Neanderthal species called *Homo pongoides*. Mainstream primatologist John Napier from the Smithsonian Institute in Washington, D.C. now became involved, but he quickly concluded that the Minnesota Iceman was a crude latex model and that there had never been a 'missing link' hominid.

Hansen, meanwhile, had an explanation: terrified of damaging the creature while transporting it, he had commissioned a model of the original, and it was this 'fabricated illusion' that Napier had examined. The publicity-shy Californian owner, meanwhile, was wary of the growing furore and demanded the Iceman's withdrawal from the public arena. The issue was further clouded since if the creature was found to have links to humans, its captors potentially faced serious criminal charges.

So was the Iceman ever more than a clever piece of showmanship? If so, has the legitimate scientific community been deprived of its right to study a vital piece of evidence of our origins? With the mystery Californian never identified and Hansen now dead, we may never know for sure. Nonetheless, an exhibit said to be the Iceman was sold in 2013, and is now on display in Austin, Texas.

FORBIDDEN HISTORY

70 LEWIS CARROLL'S LOST DIARIES

Lewis Carroll was the author of the classic *Alice in Wonderland* and *Through the Looking Glass*. Critics and biographers have speculated over the nature of his relationship with his real-life inspiration Alice Liddell. Some have argued that vital clues were contained within pages of his journals that were removed and destroyed after his death – but recent evidence suggests that they spoke of quite different secrets.

Lewis Carroll (1832–98) was the pen name of Oxford mathematician, Rev. Charles Lutwidge Dodgson. Published in 1865, *Alice in Wonderland* made him a pillar of society, but since the 1930s there have been questions about his conduct towards Alice Liddell.

Liddell was the daughter of Henry and Lorina Liddell, college friends of Dodgson from 1855. In July 1862, Dodgson took their three daughters (including ten-year-old Alice) boating and told them a story that evolved into his famous work. Relations between Dodgson and the Liddells remained cordial until June 1864, but then there was a heated dispute. In the 20th century, this falling-out fuelled scrutiny of Dodgson's relationship with Alice. That he was an early exponent of photography who took nude and semi-nude images of children has done little to help his case. Nor did a notorious photo of six-year-old Alice in a shoulder-revealing dress.

The sense that he had something to hide was heightened when some ten pages were found to have been removed from his diaries, and it now seems likely that the journals were 'pruned' prior to being donated to the British Museum in 1969. The page detailing the dispute with the Liddells was seemingly disposed of by Dodgson's niece, Violet. While many assumed Alice was at the centre of the conflict, a recently discovered note written by Violet to summarize the missing entries suggests that Lorina Liddell was upset by rumours concerning Dodgson, the Liddells' housekeeper and Alice's older sister, Ina.

By June 1863, Ina was 14. At the time, girls could marry from the age of 12, so had Dodgson developed a romantic interest in her, it would not have been illegal. Nevertheless, Dodgson was in his 30s and such a relationship would have raised eyebrows then, just as now. Yet we cannot know definitively that Dodgson was pursuing her in any way. Without Dodgson's first-hand take on affairs, we are left with a second-hand synopsis that leaves as many troubling questions as it answers.

71 THE FATE OF THE *OURANG MEDAN*

In 1952, a book published by the US Coast Guard furnished details of the strange and horrible fate of the SS *Ourang Medan*. It reported how a few years earlier the ship had been found floating in an area where the Pacific and Indian Oceans meet, its entire crew having met a terrifying end. But what happened on board has never been confirmed and, indeed, there are those who believe the story to be entirely fictitious.

The basic facts as reported are these. At some time in the second half of 1947 or first half of 1948, somebody on board the *Ourang Medan* sent a distress message in Morse code. It began: 'All officers including captain are dead lying in chartroom and bridge. Possibly whole crew dead.' There then followed several incomprehensible passages before the most ominous of endings: 'I die'.

At the time, the ship was sailing in the Malacca Straits. The SOS was picked up by an American vessel, the *Silver Star*, and within a few hours the *Ourang Medan* had been located and boarded. The crew of the *Silver Star* faced a gruesome sight. Everyone on board had died, their faces contorted in expressions of horror. Some of the victims were described as having arms outstretched as if pointing or grasping, but there was no evidence of foul play. Then a fire broke out in the cargo hold, forcing the Americans to return to the *Silver Star*. From there, they watched the 'ship of death' explode and sink, taking with it any hope of learning exactly what had happened.

If was four years before the story made it into print, and subsequent efforts to find any record of the *Ourang Medan* in shipping registers proved fruitless, leading some to conclude that the whole story is a fiction. Yet there are several possible alternatives. The ship may have been renamed by new owners but never re-registered. It might have adopted a new identity because it was involved in smuggling or some other nefarious activity. Finally, there is the possibility that someone deliberately destroyed the paper trail after the event in order to protect a dangerous secret.

Some have grasped for supernatural explanations, but any solution probably lies closer to home. One theory is that the crew were overcome by methane from an underwater fissure, or carbon monoxide from a faulty on-board boiler (which would also explain the later fire and explosion). Even more intriguing is the suggestion that the *Ourang Medan* was being used to transport biological or chemical weapons that leaked from the hold and then combusted.

What's in a name? Quite a lot, actually – especially if the name in question is that of the world's leading superpower and the story of its origins is loaded with cultural implications. America was named after the Italian explorer Amerigo Vespucci, right? Or was it? It could just be the case that a piece of cultural history that everyone knows to be true is not quite so clear-cut after all.

Many consider it an injustice that the land mass we know as America was not named after its 'discoverer' Christopher Columbus (though see page 217). Instead, so the traditionally accepted narrative goes, it was named after Amerigo Vespucci, who voyaged in Columbus's wake and made Europe aware that Columbus had not stumbled upon the outreaches of Asia as he believed, but had discovered a new continent. The cartographer Martin Waldseemüller was, in 1507, the first to mark the land mass on a map as America in recognition of Vespucci's accomplishments. However, had Waldseemüller got the wrong end of the stick? Was the name America already doing the rounds for reasons entirely unconnected to Vespucci? It is an idea that, if true, undermines a fundamental component in the creation of the American identity.

One theory, first proposed in the late 19th century, argues that the name America was not coined by European explorers but was plundered from indigenous use. Jules Marcou, a French geologist, suggested that a gold-rich area of Nicaragua visited by both Columbus and Vespucci was known by its native population as Amerrique. He even suggested that Vespucci duly changed his name from Alberico to Amerigo (a notion others have subsequently challenged). Other anthroplogists, meanwhile, have argued that Amerrique was a Mayan word translating as something like 'Land of the Wind'. America, then, becomes a name whose derivation can be traced back to the region's pre-Columbian population, rather than from later European interlopers. Such a theory is obviously incendiary stuff.

Yet adding to the confusion is a rival theory that the name originated with Italian John Cabot, who explored parts of North America, including Newfoundland, in the late 1490s. His voyages were backed by English money and his chief financier was one Richard Ameryk. So did Cabot reward Ameryk for his largesse by naming the New World after him? It is a fascinating conceit.

73 BIMINI ROAD

Beneath the waters off Bimini Island in the Bahamas, an extraordinary structure of large limestone blocks stretches for half a mile. Just what it is, and how it came to be here, sharply divides opinion. For some, it is an awe-inspiring natural phenomenon, but others see the hand of Man in its construction, with implications that there was a previously unknown but highly advanced ancient civilization present in the area.

In September 1968, three men on a diving expedition around North Bimini Island discovered what looked like a sub-aquatic road or pavement, consisting of stone blocks laid out in a long path. The stones varied considerably in shape and size, but many are in excess of three metres across. News of the discovery quickly spread. Was this the pathway to some ancient city that had been lost to the sea long ago? Or was there a more prosaic explanation for its existence?

The site has since been investigated many times, by a mixture of experts, amateur enthusiasts and the odd crank. So what are its likely origins? Those who believe that nature is responsible suggest that the 'road' is actually an extended deposit of beachrock – a mixture of sand grains, shell fragments and the like, cemented together by naturally occurring calcium carbonate.

Others, however, are convinced that this is a deliberate construction. It has been claimed that some stones exhibit tool marks, although this is disputed. Dating the rock is a tricky business but some have suggested it was built as long as 20,000 years ago. If it could be proven that an advanced race was then undertaking building projects on this scale, our knowledge of human history would be turned on its head. Some of the 'man-made' theory's supporters have even forged a connection with the legendary Lost City of Atlantis. Did that ancient metropolis lie at the end of Bimini Road? The majority of established academic research favours the 'natural phenomenon' explanation, with the consensus among geologists being that the landmark was exposed by coastal erosion around 2,000 years ago. Nonetheless, significant doubts remain. Dr Greg Little, an advocate of Bimini Road as a man-made structure (his favoured inter-pretation being that it is a harbour wall), has argued: 'For obvious reasons, mainstream archaeologists have avoided Bimini as if it was infected with a deadly virus. They have been convinced by reading others' summaries of the early research – not by digesting the actual facts . . .'

74 THE DANCING PLAGUE

In July 1518, a woman known as Frau Troffea took to the streets of the city of Strasbourg (now in France, then part of the Holy Roman Empire), dancing maniacally. A week later, she had been joined by 100 fellow dancers and within a month there were four times as many. Jigging for days at a time, many collapsed from exhaustion, and a large number died. So what caused Strasbourg's tragic dancing mania?

In an awful case of good intentions resulting in terrible consequences, Strasbourg's authorities were persuaded that the only chance for the afflicted was to let them dance it out. Drummers and pipers were brought to the city and public buildings given over to the craze. Only in September did the epidemic subside, by which time there had been numerous fatalities.

This plague was not the first event of its type, though it would become the most famous. There had been at least ten comparable incidents documented since the 14th century, including one that beset a swathe of Europe covered by modern-day Belgium, north-eastern France and Luxembourg. Historians and medics have long pondered what was behind the horrid episode. It was once believed that the dancers were followers of a heretical cult. However, this does not tally with eyewitness reports that most were reluctant participants in their relentless jigs. An alternative suggestion was that the population had suffered a mass ingestion of ergot, a psychotropic mould associated with rye that is said to induce spasms and delusions. However, it also affects blood flow so that dancing becomes all but impossible.

Perhaps the most likely explanation – as put forward by John Waller, an expert in the subject – is that the outbreak was caused by mass hysteria brought on by severe hunger and disease resulting from a famine. Physically wracked and mentally and spiritually low, the victims gave themselves over to the dance while in a trancelike state. The local population were also known to venerate St Vitus, the patron saint of dancers (whose name today is given to a neurological disorder). Yet this can only ever be supposition. The idea that ordinary people might be driven to dance until they drop is both farcical and terrifying to the modern mind. That those charged with governing them chose to encourage them in the enterprise is appalling. How those events of 1518 came to pass thus remains a dark and troubling puzzle.

75 THE ATTACK ON PEARL HARBOR

The Japanese raid on Pearl Harbor that wrought so much damage on the US navy was the catalyst for America to enter the Second World War. Had it not occurred and the US had remained out of the action, it is quite conceivable that the world today would be a very different place. But did the US President of the day know the attack was imminent – and did he let it happen regardless?

On 7 December 1941, Japanese forces launched their raid on Pearl Harbor, killing some 2,400 American servicemen and destroying or incapacitating large numbers of vessels and aircraft. President Franklin D. Roosevelt described it as a 'date that will live in infamy': a day later the USA declared war on Japan and in response Germany and Italy declared war on America. Where there had once been overwhelming public backing for non-intervention in a war that was happening far away over the sea, there was now a swell of support for engagement.

Few historians believe that the Second World War would have ended as and when it did without the participation of US forces. Winston Churchill, Britain's legendary wartime Prime Minister, had long considered it vital to bring America into the crucible of war, and had been intensely frustrated by the White House's prior refusal to commit. Certainly Roosevelt was in a difficult position: on the one hand, there is much evidence that he believed US participation was key to securing a global balance; on the other, he had to consider the strength of domestic opinion.

It is not unreasonable, then, to suspect that amid his outrage at the attack, the President might have harboured at least a little sense of relief. Here was his way into the war, and no one at home or abroad could seriously expect him to do anything else given such extreme provocation. However, in the years following the war's end, a new spin was put on proceedings. Did Roosevelt know of the attack in advance, but decide to let it proceed expressly to give him his excuse to declare war?

Numerous documents and personal reminiscences have appeared hinting that the White House wanted to 'paint Japan into a corner'. For instance, few political commentators seriously believe Japan could ever have agreed to Washington's demand to get out of China – a move seemingly designed to provoke a Japanese response. There is corroborating evidence too: Henry L. Stimson, Secretary of State for War, noted in his diary ten days before Pearl Harbor that he had spoken with the President about 'how we should maneuver them [the Japanese] into the position of firing the first shot without allowing too much danger to ourselves'. A declassified memo sent by Lieutenant Commander Arthur McCollum of naval intelligence in late 1940, meanwhile, details several strategies for provoking Japan into an act of war. Clearly, the idea was in circulation at the White House, even if nothing definite was put in train.

The question of US knowledge prior to the attack is perhaps more open-ended. It seems probable that naval intelligence picked up the approaching Japanese forces via radio intercepts, but whether the intercepts were accurately interpreted as presaging an imminent attack is unclear. And whether they ever made it as far as the President's desk is also unknown.

But it is known that the President's office was in possession of a 26-page memorandum three days before the attack, warning that the Japanese were attempting to secure 'military, naval and commercial information, paying particular attention to the West Coast, the Panama Canal and the Territory of Hawaii'. While not an express warning of a specific attack, the subsequent raid could hardly have been described as coming entirely out of the blue. Others, meanwhile, claim a large influx of medical staff and equipment to Hawaii in the days and weeks before the attack.

The argument has also been posited that Roosevelt knew an attack on Pearl Harbor was planned but simply did not believe that Japan could transport the necessary forces to break the naval base's defences – a terrible misjudgment if true. However, claims that US intelligence had broken Japan's superencrypted military codes and allowed the Pearl Harbor attack to proceed in order to disguise that fact form a conspiracy theory with little strong evidence to back it up.

Just how much the President knew or thought he knew about the coming attack is unlikely to be answered until all the relevant documentation becomes declassified. Even then, we know that much paperwork held on Hawaii was destroyed for fear of it falling into Japanese hands. So perhaps the full story of Roosevelt's foreknowledge will never emerge.

76 ELIZABETHAN OFFSPRING?

She may have had the body 'of a weak and feeble woman' but Elizabeth I famously ruled England with the 'heart and stomach of a king'. Taking control of a country on the brink of civil war, she knew she had to stamp her authority on the realm and could not be seen to be distracted by traditional notions of 'womanly things'. But did this mean she made the ultimate sacrifice, turning her back on her own child?

Early in her reign, Elizabeth, known as 'the Virgin Queen', told her subjects: 'Behold the pledge of this, my wedlock and marriage with my kingdom. And do not upbraid me with miserable lack of children: for every one of you, and as many as are Englishmen, are children and kinsmen to me.' If it was considered a weakness for a king to be unmarried and without children, Elizabeth turned it into a positive strength. But if she were then found to have a child out of wedlock, the consequences would have been dire. For starters, England would likely have collapsed into grim religious war, the Protestant church would have come under enormous strain and the Spanish Armada may not have been defeated.

It is not beyond the realms of possibility that any unplanned progeny might thus have been swept quietly off the scene, and so we come to the curious case of one Edward Dudley. Having run aground off the Bay of Biscay in 1587, he was captured by Spanish forces who accused him of espionage. His future looking bleak, he provided his interrogators with an extraordinary story. He was, he claimed, the illegitimate son of Queen Elizabeth and Robert Dudley, the Earl of Leicester – the courtier long rumoured to have shared Elizabeth's bed. In England news of this 'confession' was quickly dismissed as fanciful and all part of a conspiracy by Catholic Spain to rid England of her Protestant queen.

But was the claim so outlandish? There continues to be much speculation that Elizabeth and Dudley were lovers, so the idea that she might have fallen pregnant is far from preposterous. We know, too, that in 1561 she was bed-ridden with an illness, said to have been dropsy, that left her with a swollen belly. Might there actually have been a baby within? Elizabeth was certainly wily enough to grasp the political implications of such a situation. It is alleged that a servant of the court was entrusted with the infant's upbringing, being told that the babe was the child of a fellow employee fearful that her 'little accident' should become known to the Queen. But was Elizabeth far more central to the plot than that?

77 THE CRYSTAL SKULLS

The Crystal Skulls are a collection of exquisitely carved skulls said to derive from ancient Mesoamerica. Several reside in private collections and others belong to some of the world's leading public institutions, including the British Museum and the Smithsonian Institute, but their provenance is much disputed: while scientific analysis leaves question marks over their heritage, no one is sure who made them or when.

There are thought to be 12 or 13 skulls in existence, all different and each a thing of beauty. Some are life-sized, others miniature. A few are crafted in great detail, but others are more roughly hewn. At least one has a movable jawbone, though most do not. Even the crystal from which they are carved varies – in some cases it is intensely pure while others are smoky or tinted.

The skulls first started to appear in Western collections in the latter half of the 19th century, when interest in distant and ancient civilizations was at a peak. According to the accepted story, they were many thousands of years old (perhaps tens of thousands) and were produced by pre-Columbian civilizations in the Americas, notably the Aztecs and the Maya. Furthermore, not only were they artefacts of great beauty but they had strange powers. They could cure the sick, some claimed, or else offer visions of the future or even bring death to a desired victim. Another theory suggested that each skull was a receptacle of ancient wisdom and that by uniting them all, great (and possibly terrible) secrets would be revealed.

Initially, there was a great willingness to believe that the skulls were indeed very old and originated in Mesoamerica, despite the fact that none of the artefacts had been discovered in proper archaeological digs. By 1897, an example was on display in London's venerable British Museum, and as late as 1992, Washington, D.C.'s Smithsonian Institute eagerly accepted an anonymously gifted skull which, an accompanying note said, had been bought as an Aztec relic and more recently been owned by seven-term Mexican president Porfirio Díaz.

However, as these esteemed institutions undertook systematic analysis of their exhibits, it became apparent that science suggested the skulls were rather more modern creations than had previously been suspected. Both examples had been worked using cutting tools that did not exist until well into the 19th century, and each of the museums independently concluded that they held a recent fake. The British Museum went so far as to suggest that all of the known skulls were likely to be modern (or, at least, 19th-century) hoaxes.

However, a few diehard believers fought back. The apparent use of modern technological methods, they argued, only went to show that pre-Columbian civilizations were far more advanced than previously thought. Even more outlandish claims included the suggestion that the skulls were relics from the lost city of Atlantis, or that they were extraterrestrial in origin. A few of the wilder rumours have been taken wing in popular culture, perhaps most successfully in the 2008 blockbuster movie, *Indiana Jones and the Kingdom of the Crystal Skull*.

While it has proved impossible to find a precise date of production (determining the age of the crystal is a job beyond current technology) or establish who made them, it has been noted that many of the skulls entered the market in the Victorian period via one Eugène Boban, a Parisian antiquities dealer who had spent many years in Mexico as an archaeologist at the royal court. Noting the European hunger for Mesoamerican cultural artefacts and aware that the skull was a potent symbol in many of those civilizations, did he set up a cottage industry producing 'ancient relics'? It is tempting to believe so.

Yet, we should also give due weight to the testimony of Anna Mitchell-Hedges, daughter of the famed British adventurer F.A. Mitchell-Hedges. Up until her death in 2007, she claimed to have found one of the skulls (now known as the Mitchell-Hedges Skull) in 1924 inside a ruined temple in Belize, while on an expedition with her father. Alas, her story lacks documentary proof, and there is evidence to suggest the family purchased the skull at auction in 1943. Nevertheless, she remained adamant she had found it among ancient remains and, in addition, that it was invested with great power.

Whatever the truth, the skulls are certainly no run-of-the-mill museum exhibits. It is possible they are simply hoax creations, but for all the academic study devoted to determining their origins, we are still a long way from knowing the identity and true motivations of their creators. Even if they are not ancient relics imbued with mystical powers, they are certainly objects of compelling mystery and beauty.

78 THE AIUD ARTEFACT

In 1974, workers digging near Aiud in Romania's Transylvania region made an astonishing discovery. Next to a collection of fossil bones at a depth of just over 10 metres (35 ft) lay a large block of apparently engineered metal. Tests revealed it was aluminium, which has been produced in significant quantities for only 150 years. Its apparent presence among ancient fossils has inspired many colourful theories.

Found beneath the sand on the banks of the River Mures, the aluminium artefact weighs about 2.2 kg (5 lb) and measures some 21 x 12.5 x 7 cm (8¼ x 5 x 2¾ in). It is said to have been donated to a local museum, where it gathered dust for the next couple of decades. Eventually sent for testing at laboratories in Romania and Switzerland, it was found to be 89 per cent aluminium.

Aluminium itself was not discovered until the early 19th century, and major production did not begin to take place until decades later. Yet this artefact was purportedly discovered in a geological stratum and alongside bones from a long-extinct woolly mammoth that suggest it is somewhere between 10,000 and 20,000 years old. Nor is its age the only mystery: there is plenty of debate on its purpose too. Is it naturally occurring, or has it been worked? If so, was it perhaps part of a tool, like a large hammer head? To some modern eyes, the artefact looks like nothing so much as a pedal or even the foot of a landing gear.

Given this peculiar set of circumstances, it's no wonder some of the theories as to the object's origins are extraordinary. Was there an ancient and hitherto unknown super-race of humans who not only discovered but mined and engineered aluminium thousands of years before anyone else? Others consider the object as proof of nothing less than an ancient alien invasion (even speculating that the object was part of a visiting UFO).

Then there are those who say that the object is simply a fake and a hoax, arguing that its provenance is difficult to establish and that it is rarely if ever seen in public. Others, meanwhile, accept that the artefact was found where and when it is alleged to have been, and concede that our planet throws up such occasional anomalies. Sometimes, they argue, we simply have to accept that objects appear in places where logic says they should not. It is certain that there is something decidedly odd about the Aiud artefact, but the jury remains out as to its exact origins.

79 THE AGE OF THE SPHINX

The imposing figure of a lion with a human's head overlooks the west bank of the Nile at Giza, not far from the Great Pyramid. While we do not know for sure when it was constructed, there has long been a consensus dating it to around 2540 BC. Yet the Great Sphinx exhibits anomalies that lead some to think it is far older – was there a previously unknown but highly advanced civilization in the region?

Today, the Sphinx rises high above the Giza sands, but for most of its life it lay buried, ensuring its preservation. Indeed, much of the damage it displays today is thanks to modern man-made pollution. There is no record of who ordered construction of this monument – the largest surviving sculpture from the ancient world – but it has long been assumed that it was commissioned by Fourth Dynasty pharaoh Khafre, around 2540 BC. However, opponents of this theory point to the absence of references linking the pharaoh with the Sphinx, or indeed any historical mention of its construction. Surely, such a vast undertaking would have warranted documentation somewhere?

So other researchers have proffered radically different theories. Casting aside the almost inevitable suggestion that the Sphinx was created by ancient invaders from space, a more interesting claim was made in the late 1980s by Robert Bauval and Graham Hancock. They suggested that the

Sphinx and nearby pyramids formed part of an elaborate 'map', mimicking the stars of the constellation Orion as they were in 10,500 BC. This clearly implies a pre-Egyptian civilization capable of great feats of architecture.

Unsurprisingly, the fraternity of traditional Egyptologists has shown little enthusiasm for this notion, but arguably less easy to dismiss is the case made by author John Anthony West and geologist Dr Robert Schoch that the Sphinx shows signs of water erosion. Given that we know Giza has been arid for the entire presumed lifespan of the monument, one would need to go back to 7000 BC or earlier to find localized rainfall powerful enough to cause the supposed water damage. Again, many establishment Egyptologists have disparaged these 'Pyramidiot' theories. Yet if the Sphinx proved to be as old as some have suggested, it would force a major rewrite of human history. That is surely reason enough for the traditionalists to contend that these alternative theories are mere bunkum.

80 SHAKESPEARE'S TRUE IDENTITY

Who wrote *Hamlet* and *Romeo & Juliet*? The answer, obviously, is William Shakespeare, but was the greatest writer in the English language really who he seemed to be? There are plenty of critics, academics and lay researchers who think otherwise, and with no shortage of possible candidates, the question of Shakespeare's authorship is one of the great cultural mysteries of all time.

Shakespeare's traditional biography says he was born around 23 April 1564 in Stratford-upon-Avon into humble circumstances, and died on the same date in 1616. In between, he married Anne Hathaway (with whom he had three children) and made his name in London as an actor, writer and impresario. And of course, he bequeathed a canon of at least 37 plays and over 150 sonnets of utter genius. However, in the mid-19th century the first dissenting voices sounded, often driven by apparent snobbishness. How could a low-born man of limited education write so eloquently of historical periods, aristocratic worlds and royal households without first-hand knowledge?

One is tempted to respond that he must have had a greater imagination than those who questioned his authorship. Nonetheless, the question of attribution is a fascinating one. It is true that we know remarkably little of Shakespeare's life. Was there a concerted effort to blur the historical record in a bid to conceal the playwright's real identity? Was the Stratford Shakespeare a 'patsy' for someone else who did not want or dare to be associated with the plays? As no lesser light than Mark Twain once posited: 'So far as anybody actually knows and can prove, Shakespeare of Stratford-on-Avon never wrote a play in his life.'

Almost a hundred names have been put forward as candidates for the 'real' Shakespeare, and while a great many of them can be quickly dismissed, several names bring with them more convincing arguments. The first serious alternative was Sir Francis Bacon – philosopher, writer, scientist and statesman. His case was championed from the 1850s, principally by American author Delia Bacon, who suggested he headed an authorial group including Edmund Spenser and Sir Walter Raleigh. Keen to promote their joint philosophical ideals via drama, they hid behind the Shakespeare identity owing to the highly political nature of their work. To this day, supporters of the Bacon proposition point to distinct similarities between aspects of Shakespeare's plays and known works by Bacon.

William Stanley, 6th Earl of Derby, is another who has retained strong support since first being suggested in the 1890s. Living from 1561 until 1642, he was a well-travelled theatre owner known to have occasionally written plays in his own name. Furthermore, he had close ties with the Earls of Pembroke and Derby, to whom Shakespeare's First Folio was dedicated. Another aristocratic possibility is Roger Manners, 5th Earl of Rutland. In 1907, German scholar Karl Bleibtreu suggested Manners wrote the plays with his father-in-law, the poet Philip Sydney. However there's one rather significant drawback to this theory – Manners would have been just 16 when Shakespeare's first works were published, so he would have needed to be something of a child prodigy.

Among the most delicious theories is that the works were actually written by one of Shakespeare's most admired contemporaries, Christopher Marlowe. The author of such revered dramas as *Doctor Faustus*, Marlowe officially died at the age of 29 in 1593, after being stabbed during a brawl. Earlier in the month he had been the subject of an arrest warrant for reasons unknown but probably linked to allegations of blasphemy. Did he stage his 'murder' to avoid the authorities, only to continue his career under a nom de plume?

Yet perhaps the most viable of the non-Stratford Shakespeare candidates is Edward de Vere, 17th Earl of Oxford. Oxford was a leading figure at court, serving as Lord Chamberlain to Elizabeth I. He was also an accomplished poet and generous patron of the arts. Highly educated and brought up in one of the country's leading families, he had insider knowledge of the worlds Shakespeare described, and even undertook a European 'grand tour' in 1575 and 1576, visiting locations that would crop up in the Bard's subsequent works. As one of the most powerful men in the land, he had much to lose if he was identified as the author of the often scandalous Shakespeare plays. When expressing the wrong political or religious sentiment might cost you your head, prominent society figures were naturally guarded about what was done in their name.

Does all this mean Shakespeare of Stratford was an artificial construct? The idea is not as preposterous as it might at first seem. To be Shakespeare or not to be Shakespeare? That is the question.

81 THE BAGHDAD BATTERY

During the 1930s, German archaeologist Wilhelm Konig learned of an interesting find at Khujut Rabu, a village near Baghdad in modern-day Iraq – a collection of clay jars, each containing a copper cylinder encasing an iron rod. Konig became convinced these were rudimentary batteries: if he was right, it shows that humans were harnessing electricity at least 1,000 years earlier than previously thought.

Each of the jars is about 13 cm (5 in) long, but dating them is problematic. Konig, who was director of the National Museum of Iraq, believed them to be of Parthian origin (c.250 BC to AD 224), but others date them to the Sassanid period (AD 224 to 640). According to Konig's thesis, the jars were filled with a liquid that worked as an electrolyte solution to produce a charge – grape juice or vinegar would have served the purpose. He suggested that the electric cells could have been used to electroplate silver objects with a thin layer of gold. Certainly, there is plentiful evidence of gold plating in ancient Iraq, but it is generally believed that this was done by hand application or by 'painting on' with a mercury solution. The idea that an ancient civilization was able to electroplate is thus truly revolutionary.

In the decades since their discovery, the 'batteries' have been shown capable of producing a small current, although wilder claims about their efficiency are disputed. Some have wondered whether several jars were connected together to produce a larger current, but no telltale connective wiring has yet been found.

But if they were batteries, how did this extraordinary technology become lost again? Perhaps they were a chance invention by someone who did not understand the science behind them? Alternatively, somebody in possession of such valuable knowledge would inevitably have been highly protective of it. The ability to electroplate treasures would doubtless have made a lucky few very rich, and some have even wondered if the batteries served a semi-sacred purpose – imagine the impression made by a religious statue that gave passers-by an electric shock! Another theory posits that perhaps the batteries were used medicinally, like an antiquarian TENS machine. Some classicists hold that the battery theory is simply a red herring – but in the absence of a better explanation, and given that the jars can be made to function as such, it is a notion that should not be dismissed out of hand.

82 QUEEN VICTORIA AND JOHN BROWN

To modern eyes, Queen Victoria may seem the epitome of sexual prudery, but her intimate relationship with her beloved consort Albert gives the lie to this familiar assumption. And during years of public mourning after Albert's death, Victoria retained a passionate heart. Her relationship with her servant John Brown has come under special scrutiny – but did they really enter a secret marriage?

Prince Albert's death in 1861 left Victoria utterly bereft. It was thus decided to transfer John Brown from Balmoral, where he had served as Albert's 'ghillie', to serve as Victoria's personal groom at her beloved Osborne House on the Isle of Wight. Known for his brashness and as something of a drinker, Brown put several noses out of joint with the familiar manner he adopted with the grieving queen. Victoria, however, loved his company. They spent large amounts of time together and were even known to share the odd snifter of whisky. Victoria's daughters mischievously referred to Brown as 'Mama's lover'.

If Brown was just the tonic Victoria needed, other establishment figures found his presence most disquieting. The Foreign Secretary, the Earl of Derby, noted that the two sometimes slept in rooms next to each other 'contrary to etiquette and even decency'. Victoria only fanned the flames of discontent by referring to Brown as 'darling' in their correspondence. Tellingly, when she died she was buried with a lock of his hair, a picture of him, several letters he had sent her and a ring owned by his mother.

In 1883, Victoria responded to news of Brown's own premature death with an outpouring of grief. She paid tribute to 'one of the most remarkable men' and used phrasing that some have read as equating his death with that of Albert. But what of the marriage rumours? They seem to have been started by Scottish nationalists while Brown was still alive – and if they were looking to stir up trouble, later evidence suggests they may have been on to something.

Lewis Harcourt, a politician who served in the Liberal government of Herbert Asquith, provided some of the most compelling testimony. His father was Sir William Harcourt, who had been William Gladstone's Home Secretary. Harcourt Jr reported a story told to his father in the 1880s: one of Victoria's chaplains, Rev. Norman Macleod, had made a death-bed confession expressing his enduring regret for officiating at the covert nuptials of the monarch and her servant. If this story were true, it seems likely that the ceremony took place in Scotland, probably around 1866.

Then, in 2012, the respected historian John Julius Norwich reported that his now-deceased colleague, Sir Steven Runciman, once claimed to have turned up Victoria and Brown's marriage certificate in the Royal Archives at Windsor Castle. He is said to have shown it to the Queen Mother who, he insisted, promptly had the incriminating document burned. It is an intriguing tale, though some critics have pointed out that Runciman had an impish streak and might have enjoyed starting such a (literally) incendiary rumour.

There were even tales that Victoria bore Brown a child (or three, depending on the source!). Runciman, again, claimed that in the aftermath of the Second World War he had been at a New York exhibition by the artist Prince Henry of Hesse, a great grandson of Victoria's. There Henry was confronted by a certain Jean Brown, who announced that they were related, since she was the offspring of Victoria and John's purported alliance. According to her story, as related by Runciman, she was shipped out to America as a baby, where she lived out her days. Others also claimed that a son and a daughter were secreted away in Paris. However, none of these allegations can be substantiated.

For those who think of Victoria primarily as the plump, grieving monarch dressed all in black in honour of Albert, it is difficult to imagine her being whisked off for an illicit wedding ceremony. But we certainly know that her public and private personas do not quite tally. While her grief for Albert was genuine, she was a woman who craved companionship. After Brown died, she formed an attachment to an Indian servant called Abdul Karim (known as 'The Munshi'), which raised even more eyebrows than her relationship with the Scottish ghillie.

That Brown held a special place in her heart is beyond doubt. That she might have been persuaded to marry him is less unlikely than you might think. The historian Andrew Roberts, who has looked at much of the key evidence, has suggested that they may have made matrimonial vows without ever giving themselves over to sexual congress – that might seem extraordinary in this day and age, but would have been less so 150 years ago.

83 WHY BUILD STONEHENGE?

Rising up out of Salisbury Plain in the southwest of England, Stonehenge is one of Europe's grandest prehistoric monuments, and continues to fascinate thousands of years after its construction. Who built it, when and how are all intriguing questions, especially given the extraordinary feats of engineering required. But perhaps the most baffling question of all is *why* was this megalithic wonder ever erected?

Stonehenge today consists of intricately arranged standing stones lying within extensive earthworks laid out in the Neolithic age. The complex was built over a number of phases, the first comprising construction of a ditch, bank and series of pits (known as Aubrey holes), probably in the latter part of the fourth millennium BC. About a thousand years later, 82 enormous bluestones – some as heavy as four tonnes – were transported some 400 kilometres (250 miles) from the Preseli Mountains of southwest Wales by a combination of rollers, sledges and rafts. When the stones arrived on site, they were put on their ends to form a partial double circle.

The third and final development phase came around 2000 BC, when the even larger Sarsen stones were dragged 40 kilometres (25 miles) from an area now in north Wiltshire. These were arranged into an outer and inner circle, the internal stones being arranged in a horseshoe-like shape.

Then, around 1500 BC, the bluestones (many of which have been moved elsewhere or broken up over the years) were rearranged so that Stonehenge at last took the form that is familiar to us today.

The labour required in these various periods of construction was epic. Hundreds and probably thousands of men were needed at each stage, at a time when the entire population of Britain was a mere fraction of what it is today, and when labour was normally invested in ensuring a subsistence standard of living. So what was so important about Stonehenge that it diverted the energies of so many people over such a long time? There are, inevitably, a great many theories, some more plausible than others. It has long been argued, for instance, that Stonehenge is a temple of sorts, and in the 18th century it was commonly believed that Druids worshipped here. Although evidence points to a history significantly predating the Druids, the site might still have served as a place of religious contemplation for some other order.

Meanwhile, in more recent times it has been noted that Stonehenge has remarkable acoustic qualities, and some experts are convinced that this holds the key to the monument's true purpose. When struck, the stones themselves produce sounds of distinct musicality that carry over several kilometres. So did the monument serve as a primitive communication system, a little like the pealing of church bells?

Alternatively, was Stonehenge a burial ground for the elite? The remains of several dozen burial sites have been recovered from the area immediately around the stones, so perhaps it was the case that the great and good of this part of the world were honoured in death by interment in the shadow of the Henge, just as the Egyptians buried their most important citizens in pyramids.

Others have argued that Stonehenge served as a kind of observatory. It is well known that features of the site seem to correspond with the patterns of the rising and setting sun, hence its popularity as a gathering place during the summer and winter solstices. It is not a great leap to imagine that the stones helped our ancient ancestors to track the progress of solar and lunar cycles, to predict eclipses and plot the courses of the seasons. Another of the more credible theories has Stonehenge operating as a Neolithic health spa. The likes of respected archaeologists Geoffrey Wainwright and Timothy Darvill argue that the bluestones, brought from Wales with such effort, were prized for their healing properties, derived – it was thought – from their original proximity to healing springs in the Welsh mountains. In stark contrast, there are those who see those same stones as the equivalent of airport landing lights, erected to facilitate the eventual arrival of a race of alien overlords. Given the engineering sophistication required to transport and then arrange the stones, these alien advocates argue, such knowledge could only have come from intelligent life beyond this planet.

While the ancients have kept the secret of Stonehenge's true purpose, the monument's power to invoke awe lives on. As novelist Henry James noted: 'You may put a hundred questions to these rough-hewn giants as they bend in grim contemplation of their fallen companions, but your curiosity falls dead in the vast sunny stillness that enshrouds them.'

84 ANCIENT CONTACT WITH THE NEW WORLD

While Christopher Columbus's famous 'discovery' of 1492 certainly paved the way for colonization of the Americas, there is significant evidence that his voyages did not represent the first European contact with the continent. Viking navigators certainly found their way here centuries before – but might they themselves have been preceded by Roman visitors hundreds of years before that?

The evidence for this startling claim comes via a number of archaeological discoveries over the last century, perhaps the most spectacular of which, the so-called Tecaxic-Calixtlahuaca head, was unearthed in the Toluca Valley southwest of Mexico City in 1933. This ceramic bearded bust is thought to have been a burial offering, and was found beneath a pre-colonial building constructed in the period 1476–1510. Expert analysis suggests the head dates from the 2nd century AD and is of Roman design. If a 1930s hoax is dismissed, then it must have been buried no later than 1510 – and if prior to 1492, it would confirm a pre-Columbian European landing in America (though that in itself would not confirm that it was brought by the Romans, since it could have been shipped over at any point thereafter). But this is not the only such artefact pointing to a connection with the Classical World. For instance, since at least the 1970s, multiple amphorae (pottery storage jugs) have washed up in the Bay of Jars, near Rio de Janeiro in Brazil. Although academics tussle over their age (with some arguing they come from 15th-century Spain rather than the Roman Empire), the Bay of Jars has become a focal point for supporters of the Romans-in-America hypothesis. In the 1980s, US treasure-hunter Robert Marx clashed with Brazilian authorities who claimed he had appropriated 'contraband' objects from the Bay. He in turn accused them of covering up evidence for a Roman-age vessel so as to protect the traditional narrative of Portuguese discovery of Brazil.

Those who support the notion of Roman contact regularly cite an unwillingness to rewrite history as a reason for the suppression of evidence. Tales of other purported Roman discoveries as far afield as New England and Venezuela leave some observers convinced there is a conspiracy of silence. So far, we only know for certain that the Romans made it as far west as the Canaries – how much of a leap of the imagination does it take to accept they conquered the Atlantic, perhaps even by accident?

85 THE TARIM MUMMIES

China is traditionally thought to have made its first tentative contacts with the West around 200 BC and only forged strong ties with Europe in the 13th and 14th centuries. But hundreds of mummified bodies discovered in the Tarim Basin area suggest people of European origin settled here many centuries earlier – a new take on Chinese history that many in power might prefer to remain untold.

In the last hundred years, archaeologists have recovered large numbers of mummies from the southern and eastern edges of the Tarim Basin, in the Xinjiang Uyghur Autonomous Region of modern China. The oldest date to around 1800 BC, and the most recent to the first century BC. The area's dry atmosphere and alkaline soil have kept many of the bodies remarkably well preserved. Some have hair in hues ranging from red to brunette to blonde, and many display distinctly European facial features. One of the mummies, known as Cherchen Man, stands 1.8 metres (6ft) tall, with high cheekbones, a prominent nose and a ginger beard. Wearing tartan leggings, he looks like an archetypal Celtic warrior – a view supported by DNA analyis.

Even older than Cherchen Man is the Loulan Beauty, so-called because she was discovered in 1980 near the ancient city of Loulan. She is the mummy of a woman believed to have been in her mid-40s when she died, and boasts a head of flowing reddish-brown locks and features commonly described as Nordic. Her body was buried with provisions for the next life, including a comb, a feather and some domesticated wheat. DNA testing on hundreds of other mummies has shown similar European origins. As Professor Victor Mair of the University of Pennsylvania put it: 'From around 1800 BC, the earliest mummies in the Tarim Basin were exclusively Caucasoid, or Europoid.' A DNA-testing programme carried out in 2007 by the National Geographic Society with support from the Chinese government indicated that, over an even wider time span, the Basin was home to people from not only Europe, but also the Indus Valley and Mesopotamia. Clearly, China was open to exotic foreign interaction much earlier than previously thought.

In the accepted historical narrative, Emperor Wudi sent an emissary, Zhang Qian, westwards around 200 BC in a bid to forge an alliance against the marauding Mongolian Huns. His route across Asia paved the way for the Silk Road. While the modern-day government in Beijing is more than happy to accept this version of events, the idea that Europeans had already been living within China for more than 1,500 years has political ramifications that the authorities would rather were kept in check. This is not least because contemporary Xinjiang is a separatist hotbed, with many of the indigenous Muslim Uyghur population regarding the Chinese as hostile occupiers. In recent years, Uyghur demands for greater autonomy have erupted in several violent clashes. As such, Beijing has not been keen to over-publicize the story of the mummies: while there is little scientific evidence to suggest that the bodies are Uyghur in origin, it is problematic enough that they are non-Chinese. A number of mummies are today on display in a museum in the provincial capital, Urumqi, but they are exhibited without explanation among far more recent Han mummies, thus blurring the crucial issue of chronology.

As China strives to establish itself as a superpower, it has been careful to balance domestic concerns against its international reputation. To this end, there has been no denial of the fairly incontrovertible DNA evidence. So, for instance, in February 2010 an official report acknowledged that the Tarim Mummies possess genetic markers indicative of their having originated outside China. The government's concerns are neatly summed up in the words of historian Ji Xianlin, who wrote a preface for a book on the mummies, *Ancient Corpses of Xinjiang*, by archaeologist Wang Binghua. Having acknowledged that China 'supported and admired' the work of foreign academics in establishing the mummies' origins, he continued: 'However, within China a small group of ethnic separatists have taken advantage of this opportunity to stir up trouble and are acting like buffoons. Some of them have even styled themselves the descendants of these ancient "white people" with the aim of dividing the motherland. But these perverse acts will not succeed.'

Rarely has ancient history and modern politics clashed so demonstrably. As the battle rages over propagandizing the remarkable Tarim Mummies, truth is at risk of being the first and greatest victim.

86 THE BAIGONG PIPES

In the early 2000s, news spread of a number of pipelike objects found on and around Mount Baigong in China's Qinghai Province. Varying significantly in size, they seem to be constructed from rusty iron, which a team from the Beijing Institute of Geology have dated to 150,000 years ago. Yet human habitation in the area is only known from some 30,000 years ago, and iron smelting was mastered much later than that.

It is thought the Baigong Pipes – several hundred in total – were first uncovered by academics in search of dinosaur fossils. Many emerge from caves within the mountainside and others connect to a saltwater lake. There are still more on the lake bed and along the shore too, with some commentators discerning an order of sorts in their arrangement. A few are a little more than a centimetre or two in diameter, while others are closer to half a metre (20 in) across.

For many years, the curious discovery seems to have been disregarded by the authorities, but since around 2002 there has been growing interest in their origins. Just who could have made such items, so long ago? Clearly, it must have been a highly intelligent species, with some speculating that any suitably qualified life form must have had extraterrestrial roots. Alternatively, was there a long-forgotten early branch of humankind that had the intellect and skills to undertake such work, but whose talents were subsequently lost to countless future generations?

If that all seems too sci-fi for your tastes, there are other voices proffering more natural explanations. Were the pipes created by iron magma that spewed from the centre of the Earth before solidifying into tubular forms? Or are they iron sediments washed by water into fissures that have given them their characteristic shape? Might they even be fossilized tree roots? Expert analysis has shown traces of plant matter in the pipes, as well as features that look something like tree rings. Yet could nature really be responsible for creating objects that appear so artificial?

Thus far, no one can say for sure how the pipes were formed, by whom or what, or precisely when. They are certainly a great mystery – even more so after it was reported in 2007 that some of them have highly radioactive qualities. If it can be conclusively proven that they were manufactured rather than formed naturally, then our entire concept of human history – and perhaps even our sense of our place in the cosmos – will need to be reviewed.

87 THE MAN IN THE IRON MASK

Noted by Voltaire and made famous by novelist Alexandre Dumas, the Man in the Iron Mask was incarcerated in Paris's notorious Bastille prison from 1698 until his death in 1703. His face hidden either by a dark cloth or with an iron mask (the detail varies in different accounts), he was nonetheless treated with deference by his captors. Given these circumstances, speculation continues to be rife as to his identity.

There is evidence to suggest that the captive was held in several other prisons for years before arriving at the Bastille, and was aged somewhere between his mid-forties and his sixties when he died. According to records recovered from the Bastille by rioters during the French Revolution of 1789, he appears to have been buried under the name Marchioli. This has led some historians to suspect the prisoner was in fact an Italian diplomat called Girolamo Mattioli, convicted for revealing secrets of French negotiations to buy the Mantuan fortress of Casale. Yet Mattioli's crime hardly explains why he should have been forced to keep his identity secret, nor why his principal guard, a man called Bénigne Dauvergne de Saint-Mars, treated him with such high regard.

One take on the story has the prisoner arrested around 1670 under the name Eustace Dauger, and spending time locked up in the Pignerol Fortress in modern-day Italy – a notorious abode for prisoners considered an embarrassment to the French state. Dauger, some say, was implicated in the so-called 'L'affaire des Poisons', a scandal involving attempts to blackmail senior figures in French life amid allegations of carnal excess, poisonings and black masses.

Yet many believe the prisoner must have been someone of altogether grander origin. One proposed candidate is an illegitimate son of Charles II of England with embarassing knowledge of Anglo-French relations. Voltaire, meanwhile, favoured the theory that the Man in the Iron Mask was none other than the bastard older brother of King Louis XIV, whose existence would call the line of succession into question. Variant theories have him as Louis's twin and rival to the crown, or else the sole legitimate heir (casting Louis as the 'bastard' of his mother Queen Anne and one of her lovers). There has even been speculation that the prisoner was in fact Louis's real father, returned from exile in America and intent on extorting money. That his identity remains uncertain to the modern day is testament to the erstwhile French crown's ability to keep its silence.

88 THE BOG BODIES OF NORTHERN EUROPE

Since the 18th century, large numbers of startlingly well-preserved bodies – thousands of years old – have been recovered from peat bogs as far afield as Ireland, Germany and Scandinavia. Many of the corpses show signs of extremely violent death, and historians and archaeologists have long pondered exactly who these people were, and why they suffered such brutal endings.

I t is thought that there may be thousands of bog bodies in total, the oldest dating back to 8000 BC and most coming from the later Iron Age in the first millennium BC. Many have been preserved so efficiently that even their hair and nails have survived, while their well-preserved skin can render up fingerprints. Given that cremation was common in the Iron Age, it seems likely that the bog burials had some special ritual aspect – a suspicion backed up by the evidence of torture and violence. Of course we lack any contemporary written clues as to what lay behind this brutal ritualism. Some of the victims were hanged or strangled, while others were beaten to death or had their throats cut. Many have multiple stab wounds, including to the heart, and a few have holes cut in their limbs through which ropes bound them. This was violence beyond that necessary merely to kill. In the 18th century, some suggested that these were human sacrifices from Druid religious ceremonies. Others suspected they were dispatched to appease Nordic rather than Druid deities. Meanwhile, a counter-argument asserts that they were either prisoners, military deserters or other types of reviled social outcasts. But in more recent times a compelling new thesis has emerged: are the bog bodies the cadavers of ancient kings?

At first it seems an extraordinary suggestion, but many of the corpses indicate strapping men who had good diets and soft hands, suggesting a life devoid of hard labour. Furthermore, in certain northern European cultures ancient kings were deemed to have great responsibility to their subjects – if drought, disease or natural disaster befell the tribe, the king was held personally responsible. In an extraordinary social contract, it seems likely that these regal figures lived the good life on the understanding that if things went wrong they would pay the ultimate price. Not for these Iron Age rulers a quiet abdication and retirement. No doubt this is one tradition that later ruling classes are happy to see erased from the historical record.

89 THE PIRI REIS MAP

In 1929, a German academic working in Istanbul's Topkapi Palace made a remarkable find – a map of the world created in 1513 by Turkish cartographer and sailor Hagji Ahmed Muhiddin Piri (better known as Piri Reis). Among its many points of interest, the map has been interpreted as showing Antarctica at least three centuries before it was officially 'discovered' – could it be a record of ancient knowledge?

The map, drawn on a large gazelle-skin parchment, is inscribed with text explaining how Piri combined some 20 source maps, including one by Christopher Columbus. At the very least, it is a document that gives us huge insight into knowledge of the globe at the start of the 16th century. Quite how Piri was able to access so much valuable intelligence is a mystery in itself.

But it is the 'Antarctica' question that has caused most controversy. It is widely accepted that no one laid eyes on this inhospitable land until the early part of the 19th century, and the process of mapping the icy continent took many more years. Yet the Piri Reis map shows a coastline that some believe corresponds to that of Queen Maud Land in modern Antarctica (a region only explored from 1891). As if that was not mystifying enough, it has even been suggested that Piri depicted the coastline as it is beneath an ice sheet that has been in place since at least 4000 BC. So how might this extraordinary anomaly be explained?

Sceptics argue that the land depicted is simply not Antarctica, but an inaccurate rendering of South America instead. Not everyone is so sure, though. Was there, they conjecture, an ancient seagoing civilization who navigated this part of the world and whose maps Piri somehow alighted upon? Were there humans sailing the high seas and mapping distant lands even before the age of the Pyramids? Author Erich von Däniken even went as far as to suggest that the most likely suspects for such early voyages of discovery were extraterrestrials. Gavin Menzies, meanwhile, brought things more up to date in his book *1421*, suggesting that such cartography could only have been undertaken by the super-advanced Chinese fleets of Admiral Zheng He. These supreme sailors, he claims, discovered the Americas, Australia and Antarctica long before those who have traditionally been given the credit. Whether intentional or not, it seems Piri bequeathed us a map that created delectable mysteries even as it attempted to explain the world.

90 THE PHILADELPHIA EXPERIMENT

The ability to make objects invisible has long occupied the minds of some of the world's greatest thinkers. Although a Harry Potter-esque invisibility cloak remains far off, scientists are developing materials that aim to bend light around objects. But did the US Navy manage to do the same thing to a huge ship over 70 years ago? Even more miraculously, was it teleported across the country?

The tale of the alleged experiment is astonishing by anybody's standards. In 1943, a US Naval destroyer escort called USS *Eldridge* was, so the story goes, subject to an experiment in which it was made entirely invisible, save for the impression of its hull in the water. It not only disappeared from sight, but was teleported from its dock in Philadelphia, Pennsylvania, to Norfolk, Virginia, and back again. But the experiment, if you believe the story, ended in calamity, inflicting devastating harm on the crew.

These events are said to have taken place on 28 October 1943 at the Naval Shipyard in Philadelphia. Prior to then, it is alleged the *Eldridge* had been subjected to a series of tests and one of these had resulted in its near-complete disappearance, to be replaced by a green-tinged fog. Some claim the teleportation to Norfolk, over 320 kilometres (200 miles) away, was witnessed by men serving upon the SS *Andrew Furuseth*. After the Eldridge re-teleported back to Philadelphia, her crew are said to have been found in an appalling state – some had become embedded in the fabric of the ship, others had disappeared altogether or suffered hideous physical symptoms, while still others were delirious.

Those who claim the experiment really did happen suggest that its scientific roots lay with the Unified Field Theory. This theory seeks to use mathematics to describe the interaction between the seemingly irreconcilable gravitational and electromagnetic fields. Einstein spent the large part of his later years seeking to perfect the theory but died, the general consensus insists, having been thwarted in his quest. However, is it possible, as has been claimed, that Einstein actually achieved his goal, only to destroy the evidence of his work before his death, having judged that mankind was not yet ready to deal with its implications? And had he first shared his knowledge with members of the US defence forces? We know that he was engaged in work for the US Navy in 1943, but ostensibly this was to carry out explosives research.

The US Navy has always definitively denied there was any such experiment. Indeed, it has treated the suggestion as laughable. The *Eldridge*, it claims, was never in Philadelphia, and nor was the *Andrew Furuseth* in Norfolk at the crucial time. Furthermore, there was no programme to investigate invisibility or teleportation and, besides, the science didn't (and seemingly still doesn't) exist to achieve it. Admittedly, *Eldridge* was moored up next to another ship, USS *Engstrom*, which had been subject to degaussing, in which an electromagnetic field is used to 'hide' a ship from magnetic mines. Perhaps this fairly low-level defence work was vastly elaborated upon, becoming the basis of the Philadelphia Experiment story?

Furthermore, surely former crew members of the *Eldridge* would not have kept quiet en masse if the terrible events of 28 October had really occurred? Or were they, as some commentators have proposed, subjected to a concerted programme of brainwashing by the powers-that-be? The story initially came to public attention in the 1950s via a UFO investigator called Morris K. Jessup, who entered into a correspondence with a mysterious individual called Carl Allen (sometimes Carlos Miguel Allende). Allen claimed to have witnessed the teleportation while aboard the *Andrew Furuseth*, and although his credibility as a witness is questionable and his evidence impossible to corroborate, he nonetheless came to the attention of the Naval authorities, a fact that itself adds extra weight to his testimony for some.

Should the whole episode be dismissed as a hoax? Perhaps. Yet there are plenty of researchers as keen as ever to believe that there was a Philadelphia Experiment and it was every bit as extraordinary as its supposed eyewitnesses described. While some are doubtless cranks and others have a financial interest in keeping alive the mini-industry that has built up around the allegations, others point out with some justification that the great powers of the mid-20th century were keen to harness scientific progress for military benefit in any way they could. Why on earth wouldn't the US have been looking for ways to make their Navy disappear? Moreover, who really thinks they would be open about it (particularly if testing went horribly wrong) or would leave a paper trail for the benefit of future generations of historians? In the case of the Philadelphia Experiment, the truth itself is as hard to discern as a ship behind an invisibility cloak.

Arguably the most famous religious relic in the world, the Turin Shroud is normally housed in the underground vault of the city's Cathedral of St John the Baptist. This long rectangle of linen appears to show the image of a crucified man on both the front and back. Sceptics are convinced it is one of history's greatest hoaxes, but there is still no satisfactory explanation of how this evocative image was created.

The shroud measures just over 4.2 metres (14 ft) long and 1.1 metres (3.7 ft) wide, and shows the image of a man 'in negative'. While it has a long established history as a venerated relic, it was only with the advent of photography that the true extent of its famous image came to light, being almost invisible to the naked eye. In 1898, an Italian photographic innovator, Secondo Pia, was given permission to take a picture of the linen. As he developed the plate, he was amazed to see the image come into view. Was he the first man of modern times to see a real image of Jesus Christ? An image produced at the very moment of Christ's resurrection?

Plenty, of course, disagree with that proposition. Many base their doubts on the lack of definite historical provenance – the shroud's documented past does not stretch back anywhere close to the time of Jesus, who it is generally agreed was crucified around AD 33. We can only be sure that the relic was held at Lirey in France by 1390 (ironically thanks to a letter from a local bishop denouncing it as a forgery by a contemporary artist). Thereafter, it passed into the possession of the House of Savoy in 1453. Held in Turin Cathedral since 1578, it was gifted to the Vatican in 1983.

There is virtually nothing else about the shroud that isn't disputed. Its reddish-brown stains have variously been found to be human blood (of a rare type which, it is often suggested, had soaked into the material prior to the creation of the 'Jesus image') or, alternatively, tempera paint mixed with hematite (a mineral form of iron oxide). Furthermore, there is no consensus as to how the image of the human figure could have been produced artificially, with even the most ardent cynics reluctant to argue that it could simply have been painted on to the surface by a Medieval craftsman.

The image of a bearded man seems to correlate closely to the details of Christ's crucifixion as described in the Bible. Furthermore, the cloth apparently shows evidence of wounds caused by a crown of thorns (an element not present in standard crucifixions), as well as a spear wound to the side and cuts to the knees, as though the figure had fallen repeatedly. In addition, puncture wounds apparently from the nails that hung Christ from the cross are to be found on the image's feet and, crucially, its wrists. This is known to have been the true Roman method of crucifixion, but most Medieval depictions show Christ with nails through his palms. This telltale detail has been put forward as important proof that the shroud is not of Medieval origin.

For a while, it seemed that the non-believers had at last won the day when, in 1988, carbon-dating tests conducted at the University of Oxford, the University of Arizona and the Swiss Federal Institute of Technology suggested the linen came from either the 13th or 14th centuries, but no earlier. The shroud, it was said, was a Medieval forgery after all.

Yet still doubt remains, with campaigners for its authenticity arguing that the carbon-dating tests were compromised.

In 2014, for instance, a research team from the Politecnico di Torino claimed that radiation emitted during an ancient earthquake could have been responsible for creating a false result in the 1988 tests, and that the mysterious negative imprint of a man could have been caused by neutrons emitted during this earthquake combining with nitrogen nuclei. In short, they argued that the shroud might be just what the faithful had always claimed it to be.

Others point to the fact that the carbon-dated samples were taken from an area of the shroud that had been subject to earlier repair. The cloth had also survived a serious fire in 1532, which some argue could skew modern test results. In addition, some experts have suggested that the distinctive herringbone weave of the material is associated more with the ancient world than the Medieval one (and would have been expensive, just as one might expect of a gift said to have been donated to Jesus by the wealthy merchant, Joseph of Arimathea). There is also evidence that the shroud shows traces of pollen from plants common around Jerusalem in the time of Christ, but not usually found in Medieval Europe.

Debate over the shroud's authenticity seems certain to go on, but so far science has been unable to come up with a comprehensive explanation of when and where the shroud originated or how it was produced. In the circumstances, it is interesting to note that not even the Catholic Church has formally passed judgment on the relic's authenticity. It has, nonetheless, been described by the current pope as an 'icon', and serves as a touchstone for believers around the world. The Turin Shroud is a phenomenon for sure – but exactly what sort of phenomenon remains up for grabs.

FRONTIERS OF SCIENCE

92 THE 'WOW!' SIGNAL

In 1977, eight years after Man set foot on the moon, a team of academics were using cutting-edge technology to scan for signals from deep space. Their hope was to find evidence of intelligent alien beings but nobody really expected to succeed. Then an astronomer called Jerry Ehman picked up a printout that left him dumbfounded and prompted one of the great extraterrestrial mysteries.

From 1972 until 1997, Ohio State University led one of the longest single SETI (Search for Extra-Terrestrial Intelligence) projects ever undertaken. Its most impressive bit of kit was the so-called 'Big Ear' radio telescope, with an area equivalent to three soccer pitches. From a fixed position, it scanned the skies, relying on the Earth's rotation to focus on any given point in space for a period of exactly 72 seconds.

On 15 August 1977, Ehman started to read the fateful data printout and noted a sequence of six letters and numbers: 6EQUJ5. He immediately realized its implications, circling it in red pen and writing the exclamation 'Wow!' just beside it – thus inadvertently creating the signal's enduring moniker. So what was so special about 6EQUJ5? In short, this superstrong signal, which lasted the entire 72 seconds that it was in range of the telescope, was at a frequency suggesting it originated from a sentient interstellar source. If a little green man wanted to broadcast to us Earthlings, this is just the frequency he might use.

By studying their data, the team in Ohio discerned that 'Wow!' had come from the Sagittarius constellation, somewhere around the star Tau Sagittarii. Every subsequent attempt to re-find the signal – and there have been more than a hundred – has failed. So could it have been merely a signal from Earth that rebounded back to us through space? Possibly, but the evidence in support is not strong. Aircraft and broadcasters are not permitted to broadcast at that frequency, and neither is there anything to indicate that the signal was deflected back to Earth by a celestial body, or space debris.

Assuming that it derived from an unknown source in deep space, it is possible the signal was simply a one-off. Alternatively, it might be highly intermittent. Either might explain why no one has yet been able to pick it up again. Ehman himself has always refused to get over-excited about the 'Wow!' signal. Like every good scientist, he will not, in his own words, jump to 'vast conclusions from half-vast data'.

93 NAZI UFOS?

It is well documented that Nazi engineers were hired by the American government after the Second World War to play critical roles in projects ranging from stealth aircraft and the atomic bomb to the race for the moon. Yet it is also widely suspected that the White House suppressed evidence of technologies it believed the public was not yet ready for. Was a German 'flying saucer' one such astounding innovation?

uthorized by President Harry Truman in August 1945, Project Paperclip saw more than 700 scientists with links to the Nazi regime smuggled out of Germany and brought to the United States. It was highly controversial, opening up the US to accusations that it had unilaterally 'let off' a number of war criminals. Nonetheless, the knowledge gained reinforced America's global dominance for decades. As the war had progressed, Hitler had pushed his scientists to the limit with demands for super-weapons to secure victory. Some, including the V2 rocket and the earliest jet fighters, became well known. But there were other more outlandish plans, details of which the post-war White House was content to leave out of the public sphere. For instance, Hitler came up with a crackpot scheme to bomb London and New York with flying saucers. It sounds crazy, but there is now evidence to suggest the Nazi war machine came very close to succeeding in its aim. In

1944, the *New York Times* reported sightings of a UFO over the River Thames in London. It was said to have a bell-like cockpit at the centre of a ring of wing vanes about six metres (20 ft) across. There were numerous reports of a similar aircraft flying over Prague.

It now seems likely that these witnesses (in Prague, at least) saw the product of a project led by two of Berlin's top engineers, Rudolf Schriever and Otto Habermohl. Their 'saucer' appears to have had vertical take-off capabilities far ahead of its time, and could fly at high speeds and low altitudes. Had it been unleashed on an Allied metropolis it would no doubt have wreaked carnage and caused mass panic.

Schriever would later state that plans for the craft were stolen some time in 1945, with some observers convinced they ended up in the US. Some even believe that the 1947 Roswell Incident was not an engagement with alien life after all, but a calamitous attempt to test a Nazi-designed saucer – a project around which the authorities would understandably wish to keep silent.

94 THE TAOS HUM

In the early 1990s, a flurry of reports came from Taos in New Mexico from citizens complaining about a continuous hum or droning noise that had truly got inside their heads. Only a small proportion of the town was suffering, but there were more than enough cases to cause a stir. But what causes the problem? Is it all in the mind, is there a simple explanation or is something more sinister at play?

The enjoyably bohemian town of Taos is by no means the only place to suffer from 'the Hum'. In fact, there is a large-scale project aimed at mapping areas subject to hums around the world. Since the early 1970s, the phenomenon has been identified in dozens of locations as far afield as North America, the UK, Ireland, Australia and New Zealand.

Somewhere between 2 and 10 per cent of Taos's population are thought to hear the hum, which seems to have a frequency between 40 and 80 hertz. Research data suggests older women are most likely victims. Most describe it as something akin to having a car engine continuously running outside your home, or else like standing under a power line. It can be an unpleasant and annoying accompaniment to everyday life, but it is not necessarily hugely debilitating.

As for what causes it, an incidence of mass tinnitus has been ruled out. It has been suggested that sufferers might be experiencing spontaneous otoacoustic emissions – that is to say, they are hearing the noises that their own ears make, which most of us normally filter out amid the extravagant soundscapes of modern life. However, this does not really explain why outbreaks should be so localized.

A few outward-looking souls are convinced that the noise results from extraterrestrials busying themselves in underground bases, or even from government-sponsored mind-control experiments on sections of the local populace. Others believe the explanation may be more humdrum – the finger is most commonly pointed at industrial or agricultural equipment causing sound vibrations that penetrate the ears of selected listeners many kilometres away. It has even been suggested that the Taos Hum, like other hums around the world, is merely an auditory hallucination that took grip of large numbers of people as rumours of its existence grew.

But for now no one can say for sure what causes the hum, and until someone can, speculation as to its source will persist.

95 THE DISAPPEARING BEES

If you think the large-scale demise of our bee populations only affects those with a passion for honey, think again. Bees are instrumental in the pollination of crops around the globe that sustain us all, and since the turn of the century they have been dying in truly worrying numbers. But getting to the bottom of the problem has proved difficult, especially given the commercial and other vested interests involved.

The phenomenon known as Colony Collapse Disorder (CCD) was first noted in North America, where millions upon millions of bees died without obvious cause, often in areas where they had previously prospered. Europe soon reported a similar situation. Some 75 per cent of the world's crops require pollination, which is why collapsing bee populations cause such concern: if the bees die, some environmentalists argue, an awfully large proportion of the human population will not be far behind.

No one credibly argues that there is a single cause, but there are a number of 'leading suspects', including habitat destruction, disease, mites and parasites, the introduction of alien bee species, the growth of genetically modified crops and even the spread of mobile phone masts. However, few seriously doubt that some of the most commonly used insecticides are likely contributing to CCD – in particular, so-called neonicotinoid insecticides. In 2014, Chensheng Lu of the

Harvard School of Public Health noted: 'Neonicotinoids are highly likely to be responsible for triggering "colony collapse disorder" in honeybee hives that were healthy prior to the arrival of winter.'

But the appetite to curb their use has been patchy to say the least. In 2013, the European Food Safety Authority announced an initial two-year ban on three particular neonicotinoids, but eight EU members opposed it, citing a lack of conclusive scientific evidence. In the same year an alliance of bee-keepers and environmental groups took legal action against the US's Environmental Protection Agency for failing to institute a similar ban. The Agency responded by pointing the finger instead at the Varroa mite and suggested the blame laid at the door of insecticides had been overstated. Clearly, modern agriculture in both the developing and developed world relies on the use of pesticides supplied by a chemical industry that is both rich and influential. However, it is surely folly to allow commercial pragmatism to get in the way of resolving a problem whose consequences may prove catastrophic.

96 THORIUM FISSION

It needs hardly be said that the world faces an energy crisis. We risk environmental catastrophe by over-reliance on fossil fuels, nuclear energy has disastrous potential and other sources are either unproven or limited. Yet advocates of thorium fission argue that we have at hand a material to fuel nuclear plants that is efficient and far safer than uranium. So why aren't governments around the world adopting it?

While a growing population demands ever more energy, few of the sources from which we derive it are problem free. Thorium, however, seems to have much going for it, particularly when compared to the current leading nuclear fuel: uranium. It is estimated that there is about four times as much thorium as uranium, and supporters claim it is easier and cleaner to mine. Australia and the United States have the largest resources, accounting for over a third of the world's reserves. This would reduce reliance on politically unstable regions. And thorium compares favourably with both uranium and coal in terms of production efficiency, while creating much less waste. Its waste products are also far harder to weaponize.

In the years after the Second World War, the US government invested significantly in thorium research, running a test reactor at Oak Ridge National Laboratory from 1965 until 1969. However, in 1973, Washington closed down the research programme entirely. Other developed nations were equally tentative – only in recent times has thorium begun to get a look-in again, spearheaded by emerging economies like China and India. So why the reluctance to persevere with a material that showed so much potential?

Conspiracy theories abound, and many have blamed vested interests. For all the difficulties of energy generation, it is a highly profitable industry and leverages influence over governments around the world. Did those enjoying the rewards from traditional energy sources simply want to eliminate a rival fuel from the field, especially given sizable costs in developing it for commercial use? If financial considerations did scupper its chances, surely the question should be: 'Can we afford not to invest?' Alternatively, was its lack of suitability for use in nuclear weapons enough to lose the support of at least some administrations? It is a depressing but all too convincing suggestion. The World Nuclear Association has asserted that thorium 'offers enormous energy security benefits in the long term'. Why then is it so little known?

97 RED RAIN

On 25 July 2001, rain as red as blood began to fall from the skies over Kerala in western India. Those beneath it saw their clothes stained pink, while crimson droplets burned the leaves off trees. More downpours followed over the next two months. Could there be truth behind the theory that this unusually coloured precipitation shows we are descended from extraterrestrial life?

History records multiple instances of red rain, usually attributable to dust and sand particles picked up by rain clouds. So when Kerala experienced its scarlet shower, many expected an explanation along similar lines – if the deserts of Arabia were not the origin of the dust particles, then might they derive from a recent volcanic eruption in the Philippines? It seemed an eminently logical explanation – except that when the rain was examined under laboratory conditions, the red particles were shown to be something other than sand or dust. In fact, they had a biological dimension.

The Delhi government ordered a joint study by the Centre for Earth Science Studies and the Tropical Botanical Garden and Research Institute, which concluded that the colour was caused by airborne spores, originating from a type of algae that proliferated in the region. But even the authors of the report conceded that they could not explain the exact circumstances under which the rain clouds would take up the spores and disperse them as happened.

Then in 2003, two physicists from Kerala's Mahatma Gandhi University – Godfrey Louis and Santhosh Kumar – came up with an alternative explanation. Taking account of reports that the rain was preceded by a loud noise that might have been a sonic boom, they suggested that the particles originated from a meteor explosion over Kerala. By 2006, they had expanded their hypothesis to suggest the rain was enriched with biological matter from the meteor, that was seemingly devoid of the DNA present in life on Earth. In other words, the rain contained an extraterrestrial life form.

While parts of the scientific community treated their arguments with scepticism, Louis and Kumar have some high-profile supporters. In particular, they received backing from advocates of 'panspermia' – a theory contending that life on Earth originated elsewhere in the Universe and was brought to this planet via comet bombardment. So it may just be possible that aliens fell from the sky over India in 2001 – and that we might be distantly related to them.

98 THE BLOOP

In summer 1997, underwater microphones in the Pacific Ocean, operated by the US National Oceanic and Atmospheric Administration (NOAA), picked up an odd noise that lasted about a minute and quickly increased in frequency. Then all went quiet again. Similar sounds were heard through the rest of the summer before The Bloop (as it became known) disappeared for good. But what created this aural mystery?

Some 95 per cent of the world's oceans have yet to be explored by humans, which means that there is a lot going on under the surface with which we are utterly unfamiliar. One need only take a look at some of the curious fish to be found in your local aquarium to realize that the marine world is full of unimaginably mysterious and exotic creatures. It is little wonder, therefore, that The Bloop so captured the imagination of all who encountered it. What could possibly be responsible for creating such a strange noise? The mind boggled. Many who heard it were convinced it must be emanating from a sentient being. Yet the data showed that the sound was far louder than the song of even the largest whale. If a creature was producing it, it must either be huge, or else have developed sub-aquatic vocal abilities beyond any already known. So had the NOAA detected an awesome giant of the sea, or a smaller but highly developed new beastie?

The answer is a categorical 'maybe'. Listening posts 5,000 km (3,000 miles) away from each other picked up the noise, and a few mischievous types pointed out that it no doubt derived from the mythical Cthulhu, a creature imprisoned in the fictional southern Pacific lost city of R'lyeh according to the horror novels of H.P. Lovecraft. However, more serious analysts refused to rule out the existence of an extraordinary and previously unknown species.

Yet other scientists were unconvinced by the argument that the sound had organic origins. Instead, they suspected it was a cracking sound that occurs when an ice shelf is breaking up. In other words, rather than worrying about theoretical sea monsters, we might better engage our time by addressing climate change and the ongoing collapse of the polar ecosystem. Whatever the cause of The Bloop – and the question remains much debated – we can be sure of two things: there is much more on this planet than we yet understand, and we would do well to listen when it communicates with us.

99 THE TUNGUSKA EVENT

On 30 June 1908, an unexplained event took place near the Podkamennaya Tunguska River in Siberia. A huge explosion, many times more powerful than the one caused by the atom bomb dropped on Hiroshima, felled tens of millions of trees in an area covering 2,100 square kilometres (800 square miles). The shockwave was equivalent to an earthquake measuring 5 on the Richter scale. So what happened?

There were, incredibly, no fatalities – thanks in large part to the low levels of human habitation in the area. This was also, perhaps, the reason for the lack of immediate interest in what is now generally acknowledged as a colossal 'impact event' (almost certainly the largest involving Earth in human history). But, some suggest, maybe the authorities had good reason not to look too closely for what was responsible?

The relatively few who saw the event reported a column of intense blue-white light in the sky, followed after a few minutes by a flash and then a sound akin to artillery fire. Next came a shockwave that could be felt for hundreds of kilometres in all directions. Trees collapsed as if snapped at their base, as a blast of heat set their branches ablaze.

There would be no serious investigation of what happened at Tunguska for a further 13 years, until in 1921 a geologist called Leonid Kulik was in the area and concluded from local reports that the site had been the scene of a huge meteorite crash. It certainly seemed a more probable explanation than the belief expressed by some locals that it was an act of vengeance by the god Ogdy. It was, however, a further six years before Kulik secured funding from Moscow to further test his hypothesis. To his surprise, he could find no evidence of the telltale crater that would have confirmed an asteroid strike. Eventually, it was established that the razed forest had created a butterfly-like shadow more than 64 kilometres across and 48 kilometres long (40 x 30 miles).

In 1930, a new argument emerged, championed by the British astronomer Frank Whipple. He said that it was not a meteor that had been responsible, but an icy comet instead. The suggestion led to decades of academic debate that continues to this day. However, the current overriding consensus is that the devastation was wrought by an air burst – a body of very hot, compressed air produced by an asteroid entering the atmosphere high above Earth's surface. The asteroid itself would likely have burned up or exploded before it reached the surface of the planet, hence the absence of a crater.

Yet while the orthodox scientific community argues over whether a comet or an asteroid was behind the event, there are plenty of alternative theses. Some certainly come from out of left field, but they are not entirely without credibility. In the late 1980s, for instance, one study suggested a freak sort of nuclear fusion reaction caused by a comet entering the atmosphere. Others have posited that the explosion arose from the spontaneous release and combustion of vast quantities of natural gas trapped beneath the Earth's crust.

In the 1970s, a team from the University of Texas at Austin even made the Doomsday-ish suggestion that a black hole had passed across our planet, although many rival academics consider this highly unlikely. There is also the inevitable band of UFOlogists convinced that it was an errant spacecraft that crash-landed into the darkest depths of Russia (the Martian-mobile presumably disintegrating on impact to explain the lack of any physical evidence).

Perhaps most intriguing, though, are those who blame the devastation at Tunguska on the Serbian scientific genius Nikola Tesla, famed as the inventor of alternating current, and then working in America. There has long been speculation, fuelled by Tesla himself, that he created a 'death ray' – a beam weapon of potentially immense power. Despite his eccentricities, Tesla was a man worth listening to in matters of technology, and his death ray attracted the attention of the world's most powerful governments. Some say papers describing the weapon mysteriously disappeared after his death in 1943 – is it possible that he 'test-fired' his invention back in 1908 and, appalled at the results, promptly dismantled it?

It might seem like the stuff of science fiction, but well over a century after the incident there is still no universally accepted explanation for what occurred. Given its magnitude, it is difficult to understand why it took so long for the Tunguska explosion to be properly investigated (even bearing in mind the instability of Russian society at the beginning of the 20th century). Could it have been the case that the powers-that-be had a better idea of what had gone on than they liked to admit? Or, at least, did they have their fears as to what was responsible and decided it was best to turn a blind eye?

100 THE END OF THE WORLD

Mankind seems to like nothing more than predicting its own imminent demise – if not by flood or famine, then through war, pestilence or something else entirely. Happily thus far, every one of these predictions has been wrong: one need only think of all those who had to trudge their way back down from hill-tops ascended in the erroneous belief that the end was nigh. But presumably one day really will be our last?

As recently as 2012, large numbers of people were apparently convinced we faced imminent Armageddon on the basis of an erroneous interpretation of the Maya 'Long Count' calendar. When 21 December 2012 came and went, we were all able to breathe a big sigh of relief. Yet it would indicate extreme arrogance if our species did not at least consider the likelihood of our own extinction. We know, for instance, that such a fate befell the once-dominant dinosaurs, and in fact some 99 per cent of species that have lived on Earth are now no more. Some have even argued that our inability to locate alien life doesn't indicate its non-existence but rather demonstrates that total species collapse typically leaves no trace – a sobering thought.

Of course, the trouble with predicting our own Doomsday is that we have no historical precedent on which to base a prognosis. Accurate probability modelling would require data that simply does not exist. Furthermore, there are a great many imponderables: how might Mankind genetically develop to respond to threats? Will our examination of these threats alter their probability of occurring? Will we be finished off by something no one has even yet considered (an 'unknown unknown', as Donald Rumsfeld would have it)?

A threat to all humanity is known as an existential risk, and many of our greatest minds have conjured with the prospect. One need only note the existence of the Future of Humanity Institute at the University of Oxford, or Cambridge's Project for Existential Risk. So just how might the human race be brought down? Unnervingly, there are many options.

For starters, there is that staple of science-fiction writers from H.G. Wells onwards – the alien invasion. However, given our lack of known contact with extraterrestrial life so far, this should perhaps not be our immediate concern. An arguably more legitimate fear is a collision with a large asteroid or comet – there is strong evidence that just such an event wiped out the poor old dinosaurs. Alternatively, we know that our sun is heating up, and when it eventually swells in size and increases in brightness, our chances would not be good. A nearby supernova explosion of a much more massive star, meanwhile, could bombard our planet with deadly gamma rays (though thankfully no such stars are currently within range).

Then there are more localized natural threats – supervolcanoes, giant tsunamis, the shifting of Earth's magnetic poles, pandemics and the collapse of our planet's ecosystem (see page 244). Next we come on to threats that might be termed self-destructive, such as wars (particularly those waged with nuclear and biological weapons) and terrorism. Meanwhile, some existential risk experts are particularly concerned by the potential for unforeseen consequences of technological development – might we one day create an artificial intelligence (AI) that sets out to overtake us? Will synthetic biology deliver a disease we cannot survive? And how can we guard against future misuse of nanotechnology?

For those of a nervous disposition, it is comforting to note that there is little agreement on when the end may come. For instance, in 2013 a team of scientists from St Andrew's University in Scotland gave us another 2 billion years before the heating up of the sun would create a world devoid of oceans and lacking the carbon dioxide to support plant life. Yet just five years earlier, the Global Catastrophic Risk Conference that met in Oxford predicted humans face a 19 per cent chance of extinction over the next century – if those were your odds of winning the lottery, you'd think you were on to a good thing. The most likely sources of our demise (both rated at 5 per cent) were considered to be weaponized nanotechnology and superintelligent AI. Lord Rees, a former president of the Royal Society and a founder of the Centre for the Study of Existential Risk, underlined the increasing dangers of a technologically advanced world in 2013: 'It's a question of scale. We're in a more interconnected world, more travel, news and rumours spread at the speed of light. Therefore, the consequences of some error or terror are greater than in the past.'

But until the Day of Reckoning, we may as well sit back and enjoy the ride . . . however long it may turn out to be.

INDEX

d'Adhémar, Comtesse, 160
African National
    Congress (ANC), 137
Air burst, 253
Aiud Artefact, 202–3
Albert Victor, Duke of
    Clarence, 129
Albert, Prince Consort,
    211–13
Ali, Muhammad, 43–4
aliens, see extraterrestrials
Allen, Arthur Leigh, 144
Allen, Carl, 232
Alsop, Jane, 162
aluminium, 202–3
America, naming of,
    188–9
    see also United States
Americas, ancient contact
    with, 217–18
Ameryk, Richard, 189
amphorae, 218
Andrew Furuseth (ship),
    230–32
Anjikuni Inuit village,
    Canada, 72–3
Anson family, 59, 61
Antarctica, ancient
    exploration of, 228–9
Anthony, David, 142
anti-Semitism, 47
Armageddon, 255–7
Armstrong, Neil, 4, 8
Assange, Julian, 2
asteroid strike, 253
Atlantis, 191, 200
Australia
    Somerton Man, 145–6
    Valentich incident
        (1978), 80–81
Austria: Mayerling
    tragedy, 147–8
Aztecs, 199, 200

Bacchante, HMS, 175
Bacon, Delia, 207
Bacon, Roger, 53
Bacon, Sir Francis, 207
Baghdad batteries,
    209–10
Bahamas: Bimini Road,
    190–91
Baigong Pipes, 222–3
Baker Street bank job
    (1971), 16–17
Baker, Frank, 125
Baldwin, Stanley, 14, 15
Ball, Major Joseph, 15
Balmoral Castle 211
Banco Ambrosiano,
    138–40
Baresch, Georg, 52–3
Barrier Canyon rock art,
    67–8
Barton, Edwin J., 121
    Midnight Dreary: The
        Mysterious Death of
        Edgar Allan Poe, 121
baseball, 37–8
Bastille prison, Paris, 224
Batteries, Baghdad,
    209–10
Bauval, Robert, 204
Bay of Jars, Brazil, 218
Bayley, Dr Walter Alonzo,
    114
Beast of Bodmin Moor,
    178–9
Beaufort, Margaret, 93
Bee, The, 73
Beer Hall Putsch (1923),
    10
bees, disappearance of,
    244–5
Bender, Albert, 167
Benner, Dexter, 82–3
Bennett, Gill, 14–15

Bennewitz, Paul, 168
Bernhard, Prince of the
    Netherlands, 23
Bersinger, Betty, 112–13
Bierce, Ambrose, 85–7
Bigelow, Emerson, 98
Bigfoot, 180
Bilderberg Group, 23–5
Bimini Road, Bahamas,
    190–91
Black Dahlia murder
    (1947), 112–14
Black Muslims group, 44
Black Power movement,
    17
Black Sox scandal (1919),
    37–8
Blair, Tony, 14, 23
Bleibtreu, Karl, 207
Bloop, The, 250–51
Boban, Eugène, 201
Bodmin Moor, Beast of,
    178–9
Bog Bodies of Northern
    Europe, 226–7
Bolshevism, 13, 39–40,
    47–9
Borden murders (1892),
    141–2
Borden, Lizzie, 141–2
Bowen, Seabury, 142
Boxall, Alfred, 146
'Boy in the Box', 126–7
Brazil
    Bay of Jars, 218
    Colares Island UFO
        wave, 176–7
Bristow, Remington, 127
British Columbia,
    Canada: discovery of
    severed feet, 118–19
British Museum, 199, 200
Brown family, 169–70

Brown, Arnold, 142
Brown, Dan, 60, 62
 Da Vinci Code, 62
Brown, Jean, 213
Brown, John, 211–13
Brown, Mercy, 169–71
Buckingham, Duke of, *see* Stafford, Henry
Bulganin, Nikolai, 88
Burns, Charles and Frank, 76
Bush, George W., 27

Cabot, John, 189
Calvi, Roberto, 138–40
Canada
 lost village of Anjikuni Lake, 72–3
 severed feet of the Northwest Seaboard, 118–19
Cannon, Jimmy, 43
Carroll, Lewis, lost diaries of, 184–5
Casanova, Giacomo, 159
de Castro, Adolph Danziger, 86–7
Catherine the Great of Russia, 159
Centre for the Study of Existential Risk, 257
Chamberlain, Austen, 15
Chapman, Annie, 128
Charles, Prince of Hesse-Cassel, 160
Charles II, king of England, 225
Chatham House Rule, 24
Cherchen Man, 219
Chicago White Sox, 37–8
China
 Baigong Pipes, 222–3
 and Stuxnet virus, 27–8
 Tarim Mummies, 219–21
Chladni, Ernst, 64
Christian, Robert C., 32–4
Christie, Agatha, disappearance of (1926), 104–5
Christie, Colonel Archibald, 104–5
Church, Frank, 30

Churchill, Winston, 40, 194
CIA (Central Intelligence Agency)
 and Kryptos code, 57–8
 and MKUltra programme, 29–30
cinematography, birth of, 102–3
climate change, 251
Clinton, Bill, 23
cloud seeding, 19–20
Cohen, Mickey, 84
Colares Island, Brazil, 176–7
Cold War, 8–9, 29, 31
Colony Collapse Disorder (CCD), 244
Columbus, Christopher, 188–9, 217, 228
Comiskey, Charles, 38
Cook, Robin, 14
Cornwell, Patricia, 129
Coronet Magazine, 156
Cowan, Sir John, 161
Crabb, Lionel 'Buster', 88–90
Crater, Judge Joseph, 74–6
Crater, Stella, 74–6
Cravan, Arthur, 108–9
Crystal Skulls, 199–201
Cthulhu, 251
cyberwarfare, 26–8

da Vinci, Leonardo, 53
Dahl, Harold, 167
Daily Mail
 and disappearance of Irish Crown Jewels, 46
 and Zinoviev Letter 14, 15
Daily Telegraph, 96
Dancing Plague (1518), 192–3
Darby, Joseph, 163
Darvill, Timothy, 216
Dauger, Eustace, 224–5
'death ray', 254
Dee, John, 53
Diamond, Jack 'Legs', 76
Díaz, Porfirio, 200

Dillon, Martin, 152
Dodgson, Charles, *see* Carroll, Lewis
Doty, Richard, 36, 168
Douglas, Kirk, 83–4
Druids, 215, 227
Dubinina, Lyudmila, 116
Dublin Castle, 45
Duchamp, Marcel, 108
Dudley, Edward, 197–8
Dudley, Robert, Earl of Leicester, 198
Dulles, Allen, 29
Dumas, Alexandre, 224
Dyatlov Pass incident (1959), 115–17
Dytalov, Igor, 115–16

Easter Island glyphs, 65–6
Eddowes, Catherine, 128, 129, 130
Eden, Anthony, 90
Edison, Thomas, 102–3
Edward IV, king of England, 91
Edward, Prince (son of Edward IV), 91–3
Edwards, Frank, 73
 Stranger than Fiction, 73
Egypt: Great Sphinx, 204–5
Ehman, Jerry, 238–9
Einstein, Albert, 231
Eisenhower, Dwight D., 35
El Chupacabra, 164–5
Eldridge, USS, 230–32
Elizabeth I, queen of England and Ireland, 208
 offspring of, 197–8
Elizabeth of York, 93
Ellison, Robert Reed, 156
End of the World, 255–7
energy crisis, 246–7
Engstrom, USS, 231
Environmental Protection Agency (US), 245
ergot, 193
European Food Safety Authority, 245
Exmoor, 18–20

extraterrestrials, 34, 55, 73, 117, 200, 222, 229, 243, 256
alien autopsy video (1995) 154–5
Barrier Canyon rock art, 67–8
Majestic 12 operation, 35–6
And red rain, 248–9
and Stonehenge, 216
and 'Wow!' signal 238–9
see also UFOs
Eyraud, Father Joseph, 66

Faherty, Michael, 123–5
Faraday, David, 143
'Fata Morgana', 157
Fátima, Portugal, 69–70
FBI (Federal Bureau of Investigation), 41–2, 44
Fendley, Joe, 32, 34
Ferrucci-Good, Stella, 76
Findlay, Ian, 130
Flying Dutchman, 174–5
Ford, Henry, 48
France
    Comte de Saint Germain, 158–60
    Dancing Plague (1518), 192–3
    Man in the Iron Mask, 224–5
Francis II Rákóczi, 159
Franz Josef I, Emperor of Austria, 147–8
Freemasons, 62, 140
Future of Humanity Institute, 256

Gagarin, Yuri, 8
Gascoyne-Cecil, Robert, 3rd Marquess of Salisbury, 129
George III, king of the United Kingdom, 45
George V, king of the United Kingdom, 175
Georgia Guidestones, 32–4
Germany
    Kaspar Hauser, 149–50
    see also Nazis

'ghost ships', 174
Giacalone, Antony, 78
Gilmore, John, 114
Giza, Egypt, 204–5
Global Catastrophic Risk Conference, 257
Goedsche, Hermann, 48
    Biarritz, 48
Goering, Hermann, 98
Golovinski, Mathieu, 49
Good, Robert, 76
Gottlieb, Sidney, 29
Graysmith, Robert, 143
Griswold, Rufus Wilmot, 122

Habermohl, Otto, 241
Hamilton, Duke of, 11
Hancock, Graham, 204
Hansen, Frank, 180–81
Hansen, Mark, 114
Harcourt, Lewis, 212
Harcourt, Sir William, 212
Harnisch, Larry, 114
Hathaway, Anne, 206
Hauser, Kaspar, 149–50
Healey, Denis, 23, 24
Helms, Richard, 31
Henry VII, king of England, 92–3
Henry, Prince of Hesse, 213
Hess, Rudolf, 10–12
Heuvelmans, Bernard, 180
Hitler, Adolf, 10, 12, 39, 48, 240
    Mein Kampf, 10, 48
Hodel, Dr George, 114
Hodel, Steve, 114
Hoffa, Jimmy, 77–9
Holmes, Sherlock, 1, 16, 17
Holy Grail legend, 60, 62–4
Homo pongoides, 180
Hoover, J. Edgar, 44
hums, 242–3

Ilyushin, Vladimir, 8
India: red rain, 248–9
Indiana Jones and the Kingdom of the Crystal Skull, 200

insecticides, 244–5
International Brotherhood of Teamsters (IBT), 77
International Flying Saucer Bureau, 167
Inuits, 72–3
invisibility, 230–32
Iran: and Stuxnet virus 26–8
Iraq: Baghdad batteries, 209–10
Ireland
    disappearance of Irish Crown Jewels (1907), 45–6
    and Michael Faherty, 123–5
Isabella Stewart Gardener Museum thefts (1990), 41–2
Israel
    and Robert Maxwell, 151–2
    and Stuxnet virus, 27, 28
Italy
    Roberto Calvi, 138–40
    Turin Shroud, 233–5

Jack the Ripper, 128–30
Jackson, 'Shoeless' Joe, 37–8
James, Henry, 216
Japan: attack on Pearl Harbor (1941), 194–6
Jensen, Betty Lou, 143
Jessup, Morris K., 232
Jews: Protocols of the Elders of Zion 48–50
Ji Xianlin, 221
John Paul II, Pope, 70, 138–9
Johnson, Jack, 108
Joly, Charles, 49
Joly, Maurice, 48, 49
Jordan: and Stuxnet virus, 28
Joyita, MV, 94–6
Judica-Cordiglia, Achille and Gian, 9

Kane, John, 45
Karim, Abdul, 213

Katyn Forest massacre (1940), 39–40
Kelleher, Emmet E., 73
Kelley, Edward, 53, 54
Kelly, Mary Jane, 128
Kemp, Richard, 61
Kennedy, Bobby, 78
Kennedy, Jackie, 131
Kennedy, John F., 78
  assassination of (1963), 131–3
Kenney, Randy, 143
Kerala, India, 248–9
Khafre, pharaoh of Egypt, 204
Khujut Rabu, Iraq, 209
Kircher, Athanasius, 52–3
Kirtland Air Force Base, 168
Klein, William, 75
Knights Templar, 60, 62
de Kock, Colonel Eugene, 137
Konig, Wilhelm, 209
Korean War, 29
Kosminski, Aaron, 130
Krauthammer, Charles, 5
Krushchev, Nikita, 88
Kryptos code, 57–8
Kulik, Leonid, 252–3
Kumar, Santhosh, 249

Labelle, Joe, 72
Labour Party: defeat in 1924 election, 13–15
'L'affaire des Poisons' scandal, 225
de Landa, Diego, 55–6
  On the Things of Yucatán, 56
Larsson, Stieg, 136
Lawn, Sheila and Oliver, 61
Le Prince, Adolphus, 103
Le Prince, Louis, 102–3
Lee Jones, Tommy, 266
Liddell, Alice, 184–5
Liddell family, 184–5
Liddell, Ina, 185
Liston, Sonny, 43–4
Little, Dr Greg, 191
Lloyd, Fabian Avenarius, 108

Loewenstein, Alfred, 133–4
Los Angeles Examiner, 113
Louis XIV, king of France, 225
Louis XV, king of France, 158
Louis XVI, king of France, 160
Louis, Godfrey, 249
Loulan Beauty, 219–20
Lovecraft, H.P., 251
Loy, Mina, 108–9
LSD (Lysergic Acid Diethylamide), 30–31
Lu, Chensheng, 244
Lynmouth flood (1952), 18–20

McCollum, Lt Commander Arthur, 195
MacDonald, Ramsay, 13–14
Macleod, Rev. Norman, 212
McLoughlin, Dr Ciaran, 124
Mair, Victor, 220
Majestic 12 operation, 35–6
Malcolm X, 44
Man in the Iron Mask, 224–5
Mandela, Nelson, 137
Manley, Robert 'Red', 114
Manners, Roger, 5th Earl of Rutland, 207
Marci, Johannes Marcus, 53
Marcou, Jules, 189
Marfa Lights, 156–7
Marie Antoinette, queen of France, 160
Marlowe, Christopher, 208
Marshall, George, 146
Martin, Wyatt C., 32, 34
Marto, Jacinta and Francisco, 69
Marx, Robert, 218
Mattioli, Girolamo, 224

Maxwell, Robert, death of, 151–2
Maya, 199
  decline of, 55
  'Long Count' calendar, 255
  lost literature of, 55–6
Mayerling tragedy (1889), 147–8
Meacher, Michael, 25
Men in Black (MIB), 166–8
Men in Black (film), 166
Menzies, Gavin, 229
  1421, 229
Menzies, Stuart, 15
Merkers salt mine, 98
Mesmer, Anton, 160
Meteorological Office, 20
Mexico, 55, 108, 109, 201, 217
  and Ambrose Bierce, 85–7
MI5/MI6
  and Buster Crabb, 90
  and Zinoviev Letter, 15, 17
Miller, Captain 'Dusty', 94–5
Miller, Glenn, 100–101
Miller, Herb, 100
mind-control techniques, 29–31
Minnesota Iceman, 180–81
'missing link' hominid, 180–81
Mitchell Flat, Texas, 156
Mitchell-Hedges, Anna, 201
Mitchell-Hedges, F.A., 87, 201
Mitchell, Thomas and Stuart, 63–4
MKUltra programme, 29–31
Moon landing, 4, 8
Moran, Dr John Joseph, 120–21
More, Thomas, 91
Morris, John, 130
  Jack the Ripper: The Hand of a Woman, 130

Morse, John, 142
Morton, A.J., 61
Morton, Desmond, 15
Mothman, The, 172–3
Muhammad, Elijah, 44
mummies, Tarim, 219–21
Myers, Louie, 143

Napier, John, 180–81
National Geographic
    Society, 220
National Oceanic
    and Atmospheric
    Administration
    (NOAA), 250
Native Americans, 67–8,
    156–7
Natural History Museum,
    London, 179
Nazis 10–12, 31
    gold, 97–9
    and Katyn Forest
        massacre, 39–40
    UFOs, 240–41
Neele, Nancy, 104
neonicotinoids, 244–5
New England, 170, 218
New York Times, 27, 30,
    241
Nicholas II, Tsar of
    Russia, 47, 49
Nichols, Mary Ann, 128
Niven, David, 100
Nixon, Richard, 78
Norwich, John Julius, 212
Nuremberg, Germany, 149
    Nuremberg Trials, 10,
        11
    Nuremberg Code, 31

Oak Island Money Pit, 61
Obama, Barack, 27
Oberg, Peter, 61
oceans, 250, 257
Ogul, Little Davy, 84
Olson, Dr Frank, 31
O'Malley, Owen, 40
Operation Majestic 12,
    35–6
Operation Saucer, 176–7
Order of St Patrick, 45
Ordzhonikidze (cruiser)
    88, 90

Oswald, Lee Harvey,
    131–3
Ourang Medan, fate of,
    186–7

P2 (Propaganda Due)
    Masonic lodge, 140
Pacific Ocean: The Bloop,
    250–51
Palme, Lisbet, 135–6
Palme, Olof, assassination
    of, 135–7
panspermia, 249
Partington, Blanche, 86
Pearl Harbor, attack on
    (1941), 194–6
petroglyphs, Sego Canyon,
    Utah, 67–8
Pettersson, Christer, 136
Philadelphia Experiment
    (1943), 230–32
Pia, Secondo, 233
Pignerol Fortress, Italy,
    224
Piri Reis map, 228–9
plague, dancing, 192–3
Poe, Edgar Allan, 120–22
Point Pleasant, Ohio, 173
Poland, 39
Portugal: Third Secret of
    Fátima, 69–70
Poussin, Nicolas, 59–60
    'The Shepherds of
        Arcadia', 59
Princes in the Tower, 91–3
Priory of Sion, 60–61
Project Cumulus, 19–20
Project for Existential
    Risk, 256
Project Paperclip, 240
*Protocols of the Elders of
    Zion, The*, 47–9
Provenzano, Antony, 78
Puerto Rico: *El
    Chupacabra*, 164–5
pyramids, Egypt, 204–5

Rachkovsky, Pyotr, 49
Radziwill, Catherine,
    48, 49
Raleigh, Sir Walter, 207
Rapa Nui, 65–6
red rain, 248–9

Rees, Martin, Baron Rees
    of Ludlow, 257
Renick, Ash, 44
Retinger, Józef, 23
Richard III, king of
    England, 91–3
Richard, duke of York,
    91–3
Ritzi, Sally Lou, 75
Roberts, Andrew, 213
Rockefeller, David, 23
Rockefeller, Nelson, 30
Romania: Aiud artefact,
    202–3
Romans-in-America
    hypothesis, 217–18
rongorongo, 65–6
Roosevelt, Franklin D.,
    40, 74
    and attack on Pearl
        Harbor (1941), 194–6
Rosicrucians, 34
Rosslyn Chapel, Scotland,
    62–4
Roswell Incident, New
    Mexico, 35, 154–5,
    241
Royal Canadian Mounted
    Police (RCMP), 72
*Rubaiyat of Omar
    Khayyam, The*, 145–6
Ruby, Jack, 131–2
Rudolf, Prince of Austria,
    147–8
Rudolf II, Holy Roman
    Emperor, 52, 54
Rugg, Gordon, 54
Runciman, Sir Steven,
    212–13
Russia
    and Comte de Saint
        Germain, 159
    and *The Protocols of the
        Elders of Zion* 48–50
    Tunguska Event, 252–4
    see also Soviet Union

St Clair, William, Earl of
    Caithness, 62–4
Saint Germain, Comte de,
    158–60
de Saint-Mars, Bénigne
    Dauvergne, 224

St Vitus, 193
Salem Witch Trials, 170
Salisbury, Lord, *see* Gascoyne-Cecil, Robert
Salish Sea, 118
Sanborn, Jim, 57–8
Sanderson, Ivan, 180
Santilli, Ray, 154–5
Santos, Lúcia, 69–70
Scales, Lucy, 162
Scheemakers, Peter, 59
Schoch, Dr Robert, 205
Schriever, Rudolf, 241
Sego Canyon petroglyphs, Utah, 67–8
SETI (Search for Extra-Terrestrial Intelligence), 238
severed feet of the Northwest Seaboard, 118–19
Shackleton, Francis, 46
Shakespeare, William, true identity of, 206–8
Sheidt, Ed, 57
Shepherd's Monument, Shugborough, 59
Short, Elizabeth, 112–14
Shugborough Estate, Staffordshire, 59
Shugborough Inscription, 59–61
Siberia, Russia, 252–4
Sickert, Walter, 129
Silk Road, 220
Silver Bridge, Ohio, collapse of, 173
Silver Star, 186–7
Simpson, Chuck, 96
Smith, Will, 166
Smithsonian Institute, 199, 200
Snodgrass, Dr Joseph, 120–21
Somerton Man, 145–6
South Africa:
    assassination of Olof Palme, 137
Soviet Union
    and Buster Crabb, 88–90
    Dyatlov Pass incident (1959) 115–17

Katyn Forest massacre (1940), 39–40
    and lost cosmonauts, 8–9
    and Rudolph Hess, 12
    and Zinoviev Letter 13–15
    see also Russia
space race, 8–9
Spandau Prison, Berlin, 10, 11–12
Spangler, Jean, 82–4
Species, 165
Speller, Tony, 20
Spenser, Edmund, 207
Sphinx, Egypt, 204–5
spontaneous human combustion, 123–5
spontaneous otoacoustic emissions, 243
Spring-Heeled Jack, 161–3
Stafford, Henry, Duke of Buckingham, 93
Stalin, Joseph, 39–40
Stanhope, Philip Henry, 4th Earl Stanhope, 150
Stanley, William, 6th Earl of Derby, 207
Starlite, 21–2
Stevens, Mary, 162
Stimson, Henry L., 195
Stine, Paul, 143
Stolpsee, Lake, Germany, 98
Stone, Oliver, 4–5
Stonehenge, 214–16
Strasbourg: Dancing Plague (1518), 192–3
Stride, Elizabeth, 128
Stuxnet, 26–8
Sullivan, Bridget, 141–2
Sweden: assassination of Olof Palme, 135–7
Switzerland, 97
Sydney, Philip, 207

Taos Hum, 242–3
Tappin, Bob, 105
Tarbox, Robert, 143
Tarim Mummies, China, 219–21
Tecaxic-Calixtlahuaca head, 217

teleportation, 230–32
Tesla, Nikola, 254
Thai Silk Company, 106
Theosophical Society, 160
Third Secret of Fátima, 69–70
Thomas, Gordon, 152
Thompson, Jim, 106–7
Thomson, Jessica, 145–6
thorium fission, 246–7
Tomorrow's World, 22
Toplitz, Lake, Austria, 98
Tower of London, 91
Traven, B., 108
    The Treasure of the Sierra Madre, 109
Troffea, Frau, 192
Truman, Harry S., 35, 240
Truth and Reconciliation Committee, South Africa, 137
Tunguska Event (1908), 252–4
Turin Shroud, 233–5
Turkey: Piri Reis map, 228–9
Twain, Mark, 207
Tyrrell, Sir James, 91–3

UFOs, 166–8
    and Aiud artefact, 202–3
    Colares Island UFO wave (1977), 176–7
    Dyatlov Pass incident (1959), 115–17
    and Majestic 12 operation, 35–6
    and Men in Black (MIB), 166–8
    and Nazis, 240–41
    Roswell Incident, 35–6, 154–5
    and Tunguska Event, 254
    and Valentich incident (1978), 80–81
    see also extraterrestrials
Unified Field Theory, 231
United Kingdom
    Baker Street bank job (1971), 16–17
    Beast of Bodmin Moor, 178–9

Buster Crabb, 88–90
disappearance of Agatha
    Christie, (1926),
    104–5
disappearance of Irish
    Crown Jewels (1907),
    45–6
Elizabeth I, offspring of,
    197–8
Jack the Ripper, 128–30
Lynmouth flood (1952),
    18–20
Princes in the Tower
    91–3
Queen Victoria and John
    Brown, 211–13
Rosslyn Chapel,
    Scotland, 62–4
Shakespeare, William,
    206–8
Shugborough
    Inscription, 59–61
Spring-Heeled Jack,
    161–3
Stonehenge, 214–16
and Zinoviev Letter,
    13–15
United States
    alien autopsy video
        (1995) 154–5
    Ambrose Bierce, 85–7
    America, naming of,
        188–9
    and attack on Pearl
        Harbor (1941),
        194–6
    'Boy in the Box', 126–7
    and MKUltra
        programme, 29–31
    and space race, 8
    and Stuxnet virus, 27
    Black Dahlia murder
        (1947) 112–14
    Black Sox scandal
        (1919), 37–8
    Borden murders (1892),
        141–2
    disappearance of Judge
        Crater, 74
    Edgar Allan Poe, 120–22

Georgia Guidestones,
    32–4
Isabella Stewart
    Gardener Museum
    thefts (1990), 41–2
Jean Spangler, 82–4
Jimmy Hoffa, 77–9
Kryptos code, 57–8
Lee Harvey Oswald,
    131–3
Liston vs Ali, 43–4
Louis Le Prince, 102–3
Majestic 12 operation,
    35–6
Marfa Lights, 156–7
Men in Black (MIB),
    166–8
Mercy Brown, 169–71
Minnesota Iceman,
    180–81
Mothman, 172–3
Philadelphia Experiment
    (1943), 230–32
Sego Canyon
    petroglyphs, Utah,
    67–8
Taos Hum, 242–3
Zodiac Killer, 143–4
Uyghurs, 220

Valentich, Frederick,
    80–81
vampires, 169–70
Vanderdecken, Phillip,
    174
Vatican, 148
    and Nazi gold, 98
    and Third Secret of
        Fátima, 69–70
Vatican Bank, 98, 138,
    140
de Vere, Edward, 17th
    Earl of Oxford, 208
Vespucci, Amerigo, 188–9
Vetsera, Baroness Mary,
    147–8
Vicars, Arthur, 45–6
Victoria, queen of Great
    Britain and Ireland,
    211–13

Vikings, 217
Villa, Pancho, 86
Voltaire, 159, 224, 225
von Däniken, Erich, 229
Voynich Manuscript, 52–4

Wainwright, Geoffrey, 216
Waldseemüller, Martin,
    188
Walker, Joseph, 120–21
Waller, John, 193
Walpole, Horace, 158
Wang Binghua, 221
Ward, Maurice, 21–2
Washington Post, 5
Washington State,
    discovery of severed
    feet, 118–19
Waterford, Marquess of,
    163
Weather-modification
    techniques, 18–20
Webster, William, 58
Welles, Orson, 114
West, John Anthony, 205
Whipple, Frank, 253
WikiLeaks, 2
Williams, Lizzie, 130
Williams, Sir John, 129,
    130
Wilson, Jack Anderson,
    114
Woodville, Elizabeth,
    91–3
World Nuclear
    Association, 247
World War II, 10–11,
    97, 100–101, 151–2,
    194–6
'Wow!' signal, 238–9
Wudi, Emperor of China,
    220

Yale University,
    Connecticut, 52, 53

Zhang Qian, 220
Zheng He, Admiral, 229
Zinoviev Letter, 13–15
Zodiac Killer, 143–4